A STEP-BY-STEP GUIDE FOR CARE AT HOME

FACING ALZHEIMER'S AND DEMENTIA HEAD ON

CAROLINE de L. DAVIES & MARGUERITE BOYCHUK

Facing Alzheimer's and Dementia Head On
Copyright © 2023 by Caroline de L. Davies & Marguerite Boychuk

All rights reserved. No part of this publication may be reproduced, distributed, or transmitted in any form or by any means, including photocopying, recording, or other electronic or mechanical methods, without the prior written permission of the authors, except in the case of brief quotations embodied in critical reviews and certain other non-commercial uses permitted by copyright law.

Printed by:
Supreme Printing

ISBN
978-0-2288-9598-5 (Hardcover)
978-0-2288-9597-8 (Paperback)
978-0-2288-9599-2 (eBook)

DEDICATION

This book is dedicated to the memory of Carl Boychuk and Dr. Charles Davies.

Carl was a locomotive engineer who had an entrepreneurial spirit. His final job was driving a truck in northern Alberta. Carl began showing signs of early-onset Alzheimer's disease starting around sixty years of age. He coped with the isolating COVID-19 lockdowns and died peacefully at home (as were his wishes) with family at his side at the age of sixty-nine.

Charles was a child prodigy and was granted a full scholarship to Oxford University (England) at age thirteen. He went on to a successful career as a doctor in the British Army and later worked at hospitals in Manitoba and Alberta, specializing in anaesthesia and pain management. He retired at the age of eighty-four and almost immediately started showing signs of memory loss. He was diagnosed with brain injury dementia, thought to have occurred while parachute jumping during his time in the British Army, some forty-five years earlier. He remained at home almost until the end but, sadly, died in hospital at the age of ninety following complications from a serious fall.

TABLE OF CONTENTS

Chapter 1 STATS AND SCIENCE ON DEMENTIA 1

    Alzheimer's Disease 2
    Forms of Dementia: 2
    Traumatic Brain Injury 4
    Lewy Body Dementia 4
    Vascular Dementia 4
    Frontotemporal Dementia 4
    Other Conditions Leading To Dementia 5

Chapter 2 SIGNS AND SYMPTOMS OF DEMENTIA THROUGHOUT THE STAGES 6

Chapter 3 IS IT DEMENTIA? 17

Chapter 4 UNLOCKING ALZHEIMER'S and DEMENTIA: UNDERSTANDING PREDISPOSING FACTORS 21

    Blood Sugar 21
    Uric Acid 21
    Exercise 22
    Toxins 22
    Sleep 22
    Inflammatory Process 23
    Alcohol 23

    Repeated Head Trauma 23
    Medications 23
    Stress 23
    Sensory Stimulation 24
    Social Circle 24

Chapter 5 TRIAL DRUG TREATMENT 27

Chapter 6 SUPPORTIVE CARE OPTIONS: AT HOME OR IN A FACILITY? 30
    Person-centered Care 31
    Medicine Wheel 32
    Path of Dementia 33
    Everyone's journey is different 34
    Home Care 34
    Designated Living 36
    Long Term Care 37
    Palliative Care 38
    Hospice Care 38
    Spiritual Care 38
    Choosing a Nursing Home 39

Chapter 7 THE DON'T CHAPTER 41
    Don't Yell 41
    Don't Argue 41
    Don't Ask if They Remember 41
    Don't Tell Them That They Are Wrong 42

Chapter 8 THE LEGALITIES AND PAPERWORK 43
    Advanced Directive 43
    Green Sleeve 43

Canada Caregiver Credit... 44
Power of Attorney 44
Will 44
Bank Accounts and Real Estate 44
Accountant 44

Chapter 9 WHO WILL YOU CALL AFTER A DIAGNOSIS? ...45

Chapter 10 SAFETY FOR BOTH OF YOU 49
Guns and Ammunition...51
Tripping Hazards..51
Fall Prevention 52
Home Safety.. 52

Chapter 11 Wandering 55
Alarm Systems 57
GPS Locators 57
Dementia ID bracelets 57

Chapter 12 ELDER ABUSE... 59
Types of Abuse... 60
Reporting of Abuse 61

Chapter 13 A "WHAT IF" PLAN 65

Chapter 14 COPING WITH DEMENTIA BEHAVIOURS...... 68
Fears.. 68
Agnosia.. 69
Anger and frustration 71
Repetitiveness.. 74
Maintaining a positive attitude...................................... 78
Definition 80

Chapter 15 SUNDOWNING 80
    Suggestions for handling it 81

Chapter 16 THE POWER OF MUSIC 84

Chapter 17 TROUBLESHOOTING 87
    Walking and balance 87
    Thinking Outside of the Box 87
    Restlessness 88
    Decreased appetite 88
    Choking 90
    Administering medications 90
    Help with getting dressed 91

Chapter 18 GETTING OUT AND ABOUT 93
    Removal of the Driving License 93
    Traveling 95

Chapter 19 INTRODUCING COMMUNITY ACTIVITIES 97
    Day Programs 97
    Community Groups 98
    Respite 99
    Sleep 100

Chapter 20 CAREGIVER CARE 100
    Respite Care 101
    A Balanced Diet 101
    Exercise 101
    Breaks 101
    Mental and Emotional Health 102
    Keeping A Diary 102

Chapter 21 THE SANDWICH GENERATION **105**
   Definition 105
   Helping children cope with grandparents
         who have dementia.. 106

Chapter 22 TROUBLES IN THE BATHROOM:
   YOU'VE GOT THIS...**110**
   Incontinence...111
   Bowel Routine, Constipation and HELP...................... 112
   Fruit laxative recipe.. 113

Chapter 23 NAKEDNESS AND SEXUALLY
   INAPPROPRIATE BEHAVIOUR **117**
   Nakedness 118
   Sexually Inappropriate Behaviour............................... 119

Chapter 24 LIVING ALONE WITH DEMENTIA AND
   WHEN DEMENTIA BRINGS OUT A FIRST
   LANGUAGE **120**
   First language isolation.. 122

Chapter 25 THE DISEASE PROGRESSES........................... **124**
   Skin care and positioning 124
   Changing linens/sheets 128
   Mouth care 130
   Breathing changes...131
   Pain management 132

Chapter 26 POP GOES THE BALLOON............................ **134**
   When you feel that you can no longer cope.............135

Chapter 27 EXPECTED DEATH AT HOME FORM **137**
    Physical Changes 140

Chapter 28 END OF LIFE **140**
    Making Final Decisions 142
    Saying Goodbye 144

Chapter 29 THEN WHAT? **145**
    Emotional Toll 145
    More Decisions 146
    Grief 147
    Helping a grieving person 148

Additional Resources 151

Acknowledgments 153

Index 155

Endnotes 161

About the Authors 163

DISCLAIMER

This book details the authors' personal experiences with, and opinions about, dementia care at home.

No part of this book may be reproduced or transmitted in any form or by any means, including electronic or mechanical, photocopying, recording or by any information storage and retrieval system, without written permission from the authors.

The authors are not healthcare providers. The information provided within this book is for general information only. The authors and publisher are providing this book and its contents on an "as is" basis and make no representations or warranties of any kind with respect to this book or its contents.

There are no representations or warranties, expressed or implied, about the completeness, accuracy, reliability, suitability or availability with respect to the information, products, services, or related graphics contained in this book for any purpose. Any use of the methods described in this book are the author's personal thoughts. They are not intended to be a definite set of instructions. You may discover there are other methods and materials to accomplish the same end result.

The content is not intended to be a substitute for professional medical advice, diagnosis or treatment. No individuals, including those under active care, should use the information, resources or tools contained within to self-diagnose or self-treat any health-related condition.

In addition, the authors and publisher give no assurance or warrant regarding the accuracy, timeliness or applicability of the contents.

The statements made about products and services have not been evaluated by any provincial or federal governmental authority. They are not intended to diagnose, treat, cure or prevent any condition or disease. Please consult with your own physician or healthcare specialist regarding suggestions and recommendations made in this book.

Except as specifically stated in this book, neither the authors or publisher will be liable for damages arising out of or in connection with, the use of this book.

This is a comprehensive limitation of liability that applies to all damages of any kind, including (without limitation) compensatory; direct, indirect or consequential damages; loss of data, income or profit; loss of or damage to property and claims of third parties.

You understand that this book is not intended as a substitute for consultation with a licensed healthcare practitioner, such as your physician. Before you begin any treatment program, or change your lifestyle in any way, you should consult your physician or another licensed healthcare practitioner to ensure that you are in good health and that the examples contained in the book will not harm you.

This book provides content related to physical and/or mental health issues. As such, use of this book implies your acceptance of this disclaimer.

INTRODUCTION

Caroline trained as a State Registered Nurse in London, England. She has fifteen years of experience in nursing, including four years in the British Army as a nursing officer stationed in England and Germany. It was while in Germany that she met Charles at British Military Hospital (BMH) Rinteln. They later immigrated to Canada and got married in Winnipeg. Moving to Calgary in 1979, she spent a large part of her time raising money for charitable organizations including The Alberta Ballet and STARS Air Rescue. She got her Life and Health Insurance licenses in 1995 and worked as an insurance broker for eight years. She retired to look after Charles when he could no longer be left on his own at home. In 2021, Caroline qualified as a Death Doula.

Marguerite was a practicing Registered Nurse until 2016, when she retired to care for her husband at home when he was diagnosed with early-onset Alzheimer's. She has over thirty-five years of nursing experience, mostly in critical care, emergency and rural areas throughout Western Canada. She was a faculty member of the CARE Course until her retirement and then qualified as a Death Doula in 2021.

Marg and I were introduced over the phone in the spring of 2019. Marg and her husband, Carl, had moved from BC to

Medicine Hat, Alberta to be closer to their two sons. Carl had been diagnosed with early-onset Alzheimer's and Charles had been diagnosed with Brain Injury Dementia. With so much in common, we had an instant connection and were able to share and compare everything that was happening in our lives.

Marg is an incredibly experienced Registered Nurse, and she has been my rock on many occasions. After Carl passed away, she would insist on driving over to our house laden with beautiful meals for us to enjoy, and order me to leave the house for a break, while she took care of Charles for the afternoon. Those breaks were an absolute saving grace for me. I could literally feel the tension in my shoulders subside, and I felt that I could breathe again, at least for a while. And Charles clearly loved her visits because she would give him foot massages and pedicures and help him with his jigsaw puzzles.

Our phone calls have continued throughout our journeys with this dreadful disease and still carry on to this day, especially now with our collaboration on this book. We share laughter and sometimes tears, but above all else, we help each other to keep going. Everyone needs a friend, especially when you find yourself as a caregiver looking after a loved one with dementia. We all know of someone who is in this situation. Why not reach out and let them know you are thinking about them. I guarantee you will make them feel like they are not alone.

In this book, we teach you how to care for someone who has been diagnosed with Alzheimer's or Dementia. We share tips and tricks to make life a little easier for you. We will try to support you emotionally and share the paths we took while caring for our loved ones.

We provide a window into our lives in each chapter that shows what we encountered. Whether you are caring for your loved one at home or you are on a waiting list for a facility, we hope that our experiences will be of assistance to you.

We know only too well the incredible stress you are experiencing from diagnosis to death. This is a painful journey which will be laced with smiles, laughter and some funny moments. It is a journey that commands strength, patience and love.

Cherish every moment, even the frustrating ones, and know that you are not alone.

CHAPTER 1

STATS AND SCIENCE ON DEMENTIA

You may wonder why we have included this chapter filled with medical terminology. We felt that, like a mechanic understanding what happens when an engine breaks down, we should know what goes on in our brains when our bodies slow down and don't work properly.

The Alzheimer Society statistics show that there were almost 600,000 people living with dementia in Canada in 2020. The number of cases of Alzheimer's and Dementia is forecasted to double in the next ten years. In Canada, like so many other countries, we do not have the resources to cope with this growth, therefore we must find a way to age at home in a healthy manner.

Dementia is defined as "a group of symptoms which affects memory, thinking and interferes with daily life."[1] "Dementia is caused by damage to, or loss of, nerve cells and their connections in the brain. Depending on the area of the brain affected, dementia can have a different effect and cause different symptoms."[2]

Forms of Dementia:

Alzheimer's Disease is the most common form of dementia, and it includes about sixty percent of all dementia cases. It is a specific type of dementia involving memory loss, difficulty thinking, difficulty making decisions, as well as social and behavioural changes (also known as executive function).

There are three stages:

- ❏ Early Stage: no obvious signs or symptoms, the individual functions independently and may forget familiar words or locations of everyday objects.

- ❏ Mid Stage: displaying mild cognitive decline, (thinking, reasoning and remembering), this is the longest stage and it may last for years, behavioural changes including confusion, anger and frustration are noted in this stage.

- ❏ Final Stage: severe cognitive decline, showing a loss in awareness of their surroundings, advanced changes in their physical abilities and requiring full assistance in self-care.[3]

In the course of the disease process, widespread injury in the brain with the loss of neurons, (brain cells), occurs. When individual neurons stop working, the connections between these neurons also stop. These connections allow brain cells to communicate and pass messages back and forth. So, fewer neurons in addition to fewer connections equals "impaired brain function."

Alzheimer's which begins before the age of sixty-five is known as early-onset Alzheimer's and is present in two to eight percent of all cases.

Amyloid plaques, (extra sticky proteins called amyloid B), are formed between the brain cells, (neurons) in Alzheimer's disease. Long chains of these amyloid B proteins meet up and stick together so tightly, the brain is unable to clear them out. These plaques block the connections between the neurons.[4]

Tau tangles are the accumulation of proteins inside the neurons. Tau is already inside the neurons of healthy brain cells, but in Alzheimer's, the tau protein changes and becomes a mess, or tangle, inside the neurons. These tangles increase and cause more brain cell damage.

Studies have shown that brain cell damage has started before amyloid plaques and tau tangles are seen.[5]

Genetic research is currently being done to discover if it is partly responsible for predisposing people to Alzheimer's. The **apolipoprotein E (Apo-E) gene** makes proteins which carry fats and cholesterol in our bodies. It also regulates how much of this fat and cholesterol reaches our brains. Our brain needs fats for making hormones and for its own energy.

There are various types of Apo-E genes, and not everyone has every type. Some subtypes of Apo-E are linked with an increase in the development of Alzheimer's. This is the hereditary arm of the diagnosis.[6]

If you are forty-five or older and you have Apo-E4 or you have a family history of Alzheimer's, you should take preventative action, as documented in Chapter 4.

Traumatic Brain Injury can cause dementia thirty years after the event and can continue degrading the brain. Not all head trauma will result in traumatic head injury; it depends on which part of a person's brain is injured and the severity of the trauma. It is most commonly seen in people who experience falls, car accidents or sports injuries, and it can be caused by repetitive head trauma in sports like boxing, football, hockey and other contact sports.

Lewy Body Dementia occurs when abnormal balloon-like clumps of proteins are in the brain. This type of dementia makes up five to fifteen percent of dementia cases and presents with tremors, rigidity and hallucinations.[7]

Vascular Dementia occurs when blood vessels are blocked or damaged in the brain, causing brain cells to die. Vascular dementia is mainly recognized by slow thinking, loss of focus and difficulties with problem-solving.

Frontotemporal Dementia is a rare dementia whereby neurons and their connections are destroyed in the frontal and temporal areas of the brain. Personality, behaviour and language deterioration are predominant.[8]

Rare conditions that can lead to dementia:

Huntington's Disease is a hereditary disease that causes neurons to waste away.

Creutzfeldt-Jakob Disease is possibly caused by infectious proteins called prions.

Multiple Sclerosis is a disease process that causes the body to attack its own nerve cells.

Parkinson's Disease is a long-term degenerative disorder of the central nervous system. It occurs when brain cells stop producing dopamine (a chemical that coordinates movement). The symptoms usually emerge slowly, but as the disease worsens, non-motor symptoms become common. The cause is not known but believed to be a combination of genetic and environmental factors.[9]

Wernicke-Korsakoff Syndrome is caused by a vitamin B1, Thiamine deficiency.

Alzheimer's and dementia lasts an average of eight to ten years but can continue for as long as twenty years. It will be less time for those diagnosed in their eighties and nineties.

CHAPTER 2

SIGNS AND SYMPTOMS OF DEMENTIA THROUGHOUT THE STAGES

Charles could never sit still for very long. He always found something to do around the house or in the garden. He also loved to fish. I felt that the peace and quiet was so good for him, especially when he was working in the hospital and coping with the very busy on-call schedules. There were nights when he would come home and fall into bed at 3 a m. only to be called back to the hospital for another emergency an hour later. Sometimes he would have to do another surgical list before his on-call would be over. This meant that he would had been in the hospital for thirty-six consecutive hours. It was a punishing schedule.

I began to notice that Charles got quite agitated before going to work at his medical clinic. He would leave the house carrying several big medical textbooks. I realized later that he probably wanted to double check every medication and test that he ordered for his patients, because he no longer trusted his own decision-making ability. The faith in his own judgement had waned.

Marg could sense that something was off with Carl; a subtle shift in his demeanor. His once confident hands now struggled with his carpentry tools, and he forgot their names and purposes. One day, Marg asked him to get the drill and a 3/16 drill bit. After what felt like an eternity, he returned with the drill in one hand and a handful of screwdrivers in the other, confessing that he had no idea what a drill bit was.

Then, one sleepless night, Carl emerged from the bathroom and stood motionless in the doorway of the bedroom. Marg urged him to come to bed, but he hesitated and said, "No I can't. There is someone in the bed." Marg rose from the bed and guided him, patiently demonstrating that it was safe for him to get back into bed.

The subtle changes had begun to accumulate, stirring unease within. Trusting her instincts became paramount and she knew that something was wrong.

Changes are not always noticeable in the initial phase, but imaging or testing for protein, (amyloid), deposits in the brain can help clarify the diagnosis.

Mild cognitive impairment due to Alzheimer's will start making changes in their thinking ability and memory. This is not usually enough to affect their work or their relationships. It starts to become more noticeable when they have memory lapses over things like conversations, appointments or recent events. Task management may become a problem as it gets more difficult for them to make decisions. To the outside world they still appear to be fine, but the family will start to pick up on memory issues.

They can have a lack of sensitivity to other people's feelings, appear tactless at times or tell inappropriate jokes.

The first inkling that I knew something was wrong with Charles was when a colleague called him at home with a personal problem and Charles guffawed with laughter, instead of offering his advice. It was so unlike his usual caring and professional manner.

It is important to note that not everyone with mild cognitive impairment has Alzheimer's.

Moderate dementia due to Alzheimer's is the longest stage of the disease. At this stage they may become more confused and forgetful. They often require help with self-care, choosing their clothes and daily activities. They may show increasingly poor judgment and frustration. They may lose track of days and the current date, and they may not always remember family members and close friends. They may start to wander and forget how to find their way home.

As the disease progresses, they may experience even more memory loss. They may no longer remember their address or their phone number, and they may repeat the same stories. There is a significant change in their personality and their behaviour. They may suddenly be suspicious of people for no reason, (i.e., they may become convinced that a certain person is stealing from them). There may be frequent outbursts of aggression and anger.

With **severe dementia due to Alzheimer's**, mental function continues to decline and affects movement and physical capabilities. They may lose the ability to communicate, speak in ways that don't make sense or be unable to find the correct words to make themselves understood or carry on a conversation.

We had a speech therapist come and work with Charles every week; it helped him for a while.

They may require assistance for personal care, eating, dressing, using the bathroom.

They may experience a decline in physical abilities and may be unable to walk unaided, or hold up their own head without support. Their muscles may become rigid and their reflexes may be abnormal.

They may lose the ability to swallow or control bodily functions. Choking now may become a concern.

The speech therapist said Charles needed to stop drinking with a straw as it can cause choking. If you think about it, bending your neck over a glass to suck through a straw will cause difficulty in swallowing.

Charles was an avid gardener. Each year he would map out what he was going to grow in a large gardening diary; everything was meticulously recorded. Every type of seed was rated according to the bounty it produced at harvest. As his dementia progressed, I noticed that it became harder for him to record everything in his diary, and he would throw seeds into the ground haphazardly. Compared to past years, it was quite a mess. It was like a metaphorical look into his brain.

One day his caregiver was helping him tend to the garden. He wanted to plant potatoes. They then built the hills of earth around the plants, just as Charles had always done. Charles announced that it looked ridiculous and proceeded to stomp the earth flat! We were so shocked by the adamant way in which he handled the situation, and we burst into laughter. The potatoes were still amazing.

Signs and Symptoms of Dementia

Not everyone will display every sign listed below, and there is no particular order to these signs. After all, there is no order in dementia. Also, it is important to know that people rarely change personalities once diagnosed with Dementia or Alzheimer's.

In nursing school, we were taught that if a person had an angry and intolerant personality before they were diagnosed, they would not suddenly switch to being a sweet and compliant person after the diagnosis.

Memory loss: They may forget where they parked their vehicle or get lost when driving home.

When I look back to the last year Charles was practicing medicine, he took much longer to arrive home from work. When I offered to drive him, he jumped at the opportunity.

One day, Carl walked the four blocks to the post office to check the mail. He returned home in a panicky and frustrated state. He eventually explained that the wall was full of mailboxes!

This overwhelmed him, he became anxious and returned home empty-handed.

Repetitive behaviour: They may repeat themselves verbally, repetitive behaviour may also be present because they truly cannot remember.

Charles would ask me over and over again, "Where are the dogs?" He would also continually ask, "Where is my money?"

Carl became preoccupied with time but was unable to accurately read the clock. This created incessant questions: What time is it? What time are we going to bed? When is dinner? What time are we going shopping? What time are the boys coming home?

Now repeat each of these questions every hour.

A gradual and increasing difficulty with communication: This may lead to increased frustration and anxiety, because no one seems to understand them. They cannot find the right words to express themselves or to carry a conversation.

Some words seemed to be easier for Charles, like book, dog or bed, but most of the time his words were jumbled. He started isolating himself if we had people over or, when we were invited to a party. He would observe and listen but not join in because, he did not want people to know what was happening to him.

It is easier for a person with dementia to respond to a question with a 'Yes or No' answer. When Charles' brother would phone him from England, neither of them could understand each other. It was so sad. In the end, Charles would say, "Here, speak to Mother," referring to me, which was even more confusing for his brother.

After checking in to a motel in Halifax, Nova Scotia, we noticed that the water in the room ran dark brown. Carl wanted to handle the situation, so he went to the front office. He was unable to find the words to describe this situation and eventually blurted out, "I have Alzheimer's, so come with me." This was an important moment as it was the first time he had admitted his diagnosis. I felt proud of him and also felt profound sorrow.

Reduced ability to organize, plan, reason or solve problems: This is also known as having "decreased executive function." Patients become unable to manage their thoughts, emotions and actions.

I used whiteboards in several places around the house. I wrote the day of the week and the actual date in large letters. I used them to remind Charles of any appointments that were scheduled for that day, or any visitors who would be popping by to see him. I wrote the name of his financial advisor everywhere so that I could point to it when he asked, "Where is my money?" Our nine-year-old granddaughter got so used to this question, she would answer, "Don has all your money, Grandpa!"

Difficulty handling complex tasks: If requested to go to the bank and the store with a small list of items to buy, they may return with nothing accomplished, because they did not know which errand to do first. Having difficulty balancing their cheque book is often the first thing that a spouse will notice.

Confusion: They are unable to think clearly and are losing the ability to make even small decisions. A restaurant menu becomes a daunting task.

Disorientation: Getting lost while driving or walking. Turning left instead of right. They are unable to tell where they are, and they're unable to read the hands on a watch or clock. They will repeatedly ask, "What time is it?" Drawing the face of a clock with the clock hands in the correct position, is one of the tests done during an assessment.

When out shopping one day, I found Carl wandering in the mall parking lot. He was lost and frustrated because he could not find his truck; "Someone had moved it!" We located it exactly where we had parked it.

Difficulty with coordination and motor function: This is due to damage to the part of the brain that coordinates balance and voluntary movements.

Loss of or decreased sensory functions: Loss of smell, a metallic taste in the mouth and reduced visual perception, may be common as the disease progresses.

Charles had cataracts removed from both eyes in 2018. Having worn glasses for most of his life, he could not get used to going without, so he wore over the counter reading glasses all day long. I wondered about his depth perception and whether it could possibly have caused some of his falls.

Carl wore hearing aids, and one day I found him smashing them to pieces. He threw them out saying, "I don't know what these stupid things are." The volume on the television became noticeably louder.

Inability to identify objects and people: This eventually leads to the inability to recognize family members.

Carl found a crowbar in our garage and asked, "What is this heavy thing and why do we have this thing? What is it for?"

Changes in personality and behaviour, sometimes becoming obsessive-compulsive: There may be outbursts of anger, sadness, mood swings, lack of emotion and interest in what is going on around them, and in some cases, inappropriate behaviour.

Charles would often say, "I am going mad! I can't do anything," until he got busy with his word find book or his puzzle, which distracted him.

Carl had placed a beer mug on a shelf. I picked it up to look at the logo and then replaced the mug on the shelf. Apparently, I had not replaced it in the exact position that he had. He instantly became angry and yelled at me to not touch his things. This behavior was truly out of character for him.

I found that if I could laugh and get Carl laughing, his mood would improve and life would become tolerable once again. These personality changes would come and go and vary in intensity. One day Carl would be sad and angry and the next day he would be cheerful, easy to direct and get along with.

It is impossible to escape Alzheimer's disease because their every question, their every comment, reinforces and strengthens the diagnosis.

Over time these signs will worsen and will include a decrease in their speech, appetite, fluid intake and ability to swallow. Walking, mobilization and social skills will also be compromised.

Common causes of death

Pneumonia is an infection in the lungs that may lead to shortness of breath, a productive wet cough and fevers. Pneumonia may be caused by the aspiration of food or fluids. You may notice frequent coughing or choking, especially when attempting to swallow.

Dehydration is having an inadequate amount of fluids in the body, and is caused by a decreasing intake of food and fluids, especially water. You may notice dry and flaky skin, a dry mouth and a habit of clicking their tongue. Dehydration will cause a decrease in urine output and the urine will be dark in colour and concentrated.

Malnutrition results from a decreasing appetite and difficulty swallowing. This reduces the nutrients in their body and they are unable to maintain a healthy state.

Falls can lead to a variety of trauma-related issues including fractures, internal injuries and head injuries.

Infections can be caused by any of the above conditions alone or in combination, (pneumonia and urinary tract infections are the most common). Infections lead to fevers, further dehydration and signs of quickly worsening dementia.

Conrad and Brian saw changes in their Dad's mood, actions and behaviour. They felt that their Dad no longer recognized them. Conversations had changed and they worried about Marg's safety. There was pain in knowing.

CHAPTER 3

IS IT DEMENTIA?

At the beginning we all tend to be in denial.

Caroline and Marg knew there was something wrong, but they found that admitting to themselves that their husbands could have Alzheimer's or Dementia was torture. They felt that they were no longer important to their loved ones. They missed the hugs, the love and their wry sense of humour. They realized that they were becoming caregivers, no longer a spouse or mate.

I made an appointment for Charles to see his GP. The doctor felt I was worrying unnecessarily but said he would run a few tests on him. A nurse came in with a bunch of papers, and it was obvious that this was her first time doing these tests; she seemed quite flustered. I remember Charles watching her as she kept referring to the instructions.

"I don't know what is going on with me," he said, "but I am a bit worried about you!"

Everyone laughed and the testing continued. He was asked to count back from a hundred by sevens. Of course, he aced that part of the test without errors and in record time.

Other causes of memory loss or behavioural changes must be ruled out by your physician before a diagnosis of Alzheimer's or Dementia can be made, as they have similar symptoms. These include but are not limited to:

- ❑ Are they dehydrated?
- ❑ Do they have signs of an electrolyte imbalance?
- ❑ Do they have signs of an infectious process going on?
- ❑ Do they have Lyme disease?

How are Alzheimer's and Dementia diagnosed?

Examinations and assessments must be performed by your family doctor. It may take a few visits to the doctor because, a trend needs to be established and a pattern noted of the memory and skills lost.

A detailed medical and behavioural history will be taken and repeated. Questions about family history of memory impairment, (the heredity component), will be asked. A detailed personal history, activity, exercise, diet, sleep, social skills and quality of life will be asked.

Keep a timeline of behavioural changes.

- ❑ What changed?
- ❑ When did it change? Keep detailed examples.

We strongly advise you to keep detailed notes on behavioural, mood and emotional changes. These notes will be of great help when a diagnosis is in progress, so bring them with you to the doctor's office. And trust your gut. If you think a certain behaviour is "not like him/her" or know that something is wrong, trust your instincts and persevere until you are satisfied with the explanations. Taking notes throughout this journey will help you cope.

Mini-mental and Montreal Cognitive Assessment (MoCA) tests, are diagnostic written tests that are performed in the doctor's office and under the supervision of medical staff. These tests are repeated periodically to establish a trend and to assess the progress of the disease. The MoCA tests are a sensitive tool in detecting early cognitive impairment. They test language, memory, reasoning and orientation skills.

For example, the person being tested may be asked to remember three words, given to them at the beginning of the test. A few minutes into the test, they are asked to recall the three words, and probably again at the end of the test. They are asked to draw the face of a clock, with the hands of the clock drawn to indicate a specific time.

Eventually, a consultation with a Gerontologist will be made. Based on their findings, a CT scan or MRI may be ordered so that tumors, brain bleeds or strokes can be ruled out.

Blood tests will be ordered to check for infections, electrolyte balance, hydration levels and deficiencies. They will also check blood sugar levels, uric acid and perform a urine test.

Many Gerontologists, (perhaps all), will separate you and your spouse when you arrive at the office. This is normal and done in order to offer you some privacy, in the event that there are issues that you wish to discuss. While you are sharing with the doctor, your loved one will be writing the mini mental and/or MoCA tests under the supervision of office staff. So don't worry, your spouse will not be left alone.

Charles didn't do as well on the memory tests. When he had completed the MoCA testing, his GP, who was also a friend, came to reassure me that Charles was in amazing shape for his age. My gut told me differently, and I asked him to refer Charles to a Gerontologist. I knew there was something not right, and a few weeks later, my worst fears were confirmed.

CHAPTER 4

UNLOCKING ALZHEIMER'S and DEMENTIA: UNDERSTANDING PREDISPOSING FACTORS

"If genes load the gun then choices pull the trigger!"

What did we do wrong? We exercised, ate a healthy diet and took multivitamins. How did we end up here? What can we suggest to our family and friends to avoid the same diagnosis?

Studies are proving that our lifestyle and habits influence the rising rates of Alzheimer's and Dementia. These are the factors that we have some degree of control over.

High blood sugar levels: Due to poorly controlled diabetes, a diet too high in sugars, or the development of insulin resistance over time, will damage the blood vessels in the brain and lead to brain cell death. Forty percent of people with Alzheimer's have chronically raised insulin levels. In fact, diabetes has now been named Level Three Dementia.

High levels of uric acid: Uric acid is a natural waste product which comes from eating foods which contain high levels of purine such as organ meats, liver, kidney and heart, red meat, pork and lamb, shellfish, anchovies, sardines and beer to name a few.

There are two types of purines: endogenous and exogenous. Exogenous purines are absorbed by the body through the food that you eat. The endogenous purines are made by the body.

Uric acid is formed when the purines are broken down in the digestive system. A diet too rich in purines can cause a build-up of uric acid. If the uric acid remains in the body for too long, it can crystallize and cause health issues such as gout, kidney stones, diabetes and Alzheimer's.

A uric acid level below 5.5 is within normal range and should be sought after. An elevated uric acid level signals a "warning sign" in the body.

To assist the body in excreting excess uric acid, drink three litres of water per day.[10]

Lack of exercise: A good workout, a brisk walk, an elliptical or treadmill workout will increase your heart rate and deliver oxygen and nutrients to your brain. A lack of activity means less food, nutrients, blood supply and oxygen to the brain.

Exposure to toxins: From air pollution to toxins in our food, (due to some preservatives and flavour additives), all toxins will damage brain cells.

Quality and quantity of sleep: You need sleep to clear out the brain toxins which have accumulated throughout the day. You need deep REM sleep in a dark room so that the brain recognizes that it is night time. Sleep apnea occurs when low oxygen levels in your brain wake you up often, in order to increase your breathing. This prevents you from having a healing sleep, so it needs to be corrected if found to be present.

Infections: An inflammatory response is the result of an infection anywhere in your body. The chemicals released from the inflammatory response also circulate to the brain and may cause inflammatory changes there as well.

Excessive alcohol use: Alcohol causes brain damage by destroying brain cells, therefore, more alcohol use equals more damage.[11] Think of alcohol as a toxin.

Repetitive head trauma: Concussions and/or repeated blows to the head increases your risk of developing dementia.

Medications: Over-the-counter medications containing diphenhydramine (e.g., Benadryl). Please discuss the use of sedatives and sleeping pills with your doctor. Remember that taking the occasional allergy medication will help you through your day and not lead to debilitating conditions. It is the abuse of these medications which can lead to problems.[12]

Stress: Whether post-traumatic stress disorder, (PTSD), or the stress you are under on a regular basis, stress will increase inflammatory changes and blood pressure, thereby increasing brain cell damage. Developing relaxation and meditative habits, (deep breathing, yoga, mindfulness), reduces the stress response.

Dr. Heather Sandison recommends caregivers practice self-compassion to reduce the feelings of being burdened. Be gentle with yourself. Enjoy every day and try not to worry about the tomorrows. This habit will reduce stress and your blood pressure.

Dr. Kat Toops offers an easy introductory meditation exercise for beginners to practice. Take a deep breath in through your nose and exhale through your mouth. Repeat the deep breathing a few times. Relax. Concentrate on your slow, rhythmic pattern of breathing. Now think of someone you love. Relax. Breathe slowly and deeply.

Lack of sensory stimulation: If you have decreased vision or hearing, the nerve patterns in your brain will also be decreased from lack of use, so the brain connections shut down. Check your hearing and vision routinely in order to keep these brain cell connections active and healthy.

Social circle: Your community is your group of friends and family with whom you need to share, lean on, provide support to, laugh with, cry with and even get angry or frustrated with at times. They keep you motivated, give you a reason to get out of bed in the morning and consequently decrease your inflammatory triggers. Loneliness is a known risk factor for dementia. You need to seek out people. Commit yourself to finding your community.

Dr. Ryan Greene states that we are meant to be together and not isolated. This togetherness provides support, decreases loneliness and helps us connect with each other. He also reminds us that this community can be found in seniors' groups as well as religious groups.

Dr. Sid O'Bryant from the University of North Texas shares with us that people with depression, who are living in areas of socio-cultural deprivation, have an increased likelihood of showing memory loss and developing Alzheimer's. He also believes that a healthy brain requires mental, physical and social activity as well as proper nutrition.

Diet: A diet high in sugars, refined carbohydrates, (white flour), processed meats, (salted, smoked and cured meats), deep fried foods, margarine, shortening and lard is referred to as a high inflammatory diet.

Your immune system becomes activated when your body recognizes anything foreign. This triggers a process called inflammation. When the body is in a state of chronic inflammation it leads to chronic diseases, coronary artery disease, hypertension, diabetes, depression, cancers and Alzheimer's.

A diet high in fruits, vegetables, nuts, lean meats and good fats, (olive oil and avocados), is advised. Foods that will lower inflammation include tomatoes, olive oil, green leafy vegetables like spinach and kale, nuts, fish and fruits like strawberries, apples, oranges and blueberries.[13]

A healthy diet combined with exercise, (even if only walking), actively working on de-stressing and getting some good sleep, can help undo some of the chronic inflammatory changes that have occurred.

Dr. Ryan Greene reminds us that "We are what we eat!" If we ingest unhealthy food, it will cause a depressed immune system, which leads to disease and increased inflammatory states.

Brain exercises: An excellent way to keep your mind fresh is to practise brain exercises. Walking backwards is one suggestion. It is also good for your heart and improves your balance.

Try using your non-dominant hand to brush your teeth. It is supposed to increase and strengthen connections between the two hemispheres of the brain. (It is harder than you think at the beginning!)

Balancing on one leg for twenty to thirty seconds and then repeating it on the other leg, is great for the brain. According to Dr. Michael Mosley, every time you stand on one leg, it is an opportunity to recalibrate your brain, form new connections and strengthen the coordination between your ears, eyes, joints and muscles. More information is available at bbc.co.uk under the title of *Just One Thing with Michael Mosley* on BBC4.

You can get really brave and try brushing your teeth with the non-dominant hand and standing on one leg at the same time, but make sure you have something to grab on to at the beginning!

Any aerobic exercise or movement, (even dancing), will stimulate your brain through specific repetitive movements, and will increase the amount of oxygen delivered to the brain throughout the workout.

Everything in moderation would apply in this chapter. An excess of anything could tip the scales and become unhealthy. We must enjoy life with a smile and a positive attitude.

CHAPTER 5

TRIAL DRUG TREATMENT

It is natural to want to try any drug which may delay the onset of dementia. Trials are few and far between, and, to be honest, none of these trials have shown great success. They come with side effects, but most of us would be prepared to take the risk. We grasp at any straw.

Carl's Gerontologist suggested a trial period of a drug called Galantamine in the hopes that it would slow the progress of the disease. Galantamine is used to treat mild to moderate memory loss and mental changes associated with Alzheimer's. This drug is not fully covered by Medicare, so please check with your pharmacist regarding costs as it varies from province to province.

Was Galantamine effective for Carl? I don't know. The disease continued to progress. Would it have progressed faster without the drug? Who knows.

Charles' Dementia was too advanced to attempt trial drugs. He was put on antipsychotics during his first hospital admission. This kept him sedated for long periods at a time. Unfortunately, his body seemed to adapt to this drug fairly quickly, so the dose was constantly being increased to keep him quiet and prevent him from trying to get out of bed. I wish there had been something else they could have prescribed in its place. He was so drugged up and confused. I asked for him to be discharged to my care as soon as it was possible.

I was very fortunate to have a private nurse to help me both day and night because Charles rarely slept soundly. But he was definitely less fractious when he was in familiar surroundings.

To date, drugs have not been the success that everyone had hoped for. Newer drugs are offering a decline or a slowing down of the progression of the disease, but it is not a reversal or cure. While Lecanemab is not yet available in Canada, some doctors in the US are administering the drug and are excited with initial results. There is now a new blood test which reveals proteins and evidence of tao tangles and amyloid plaques, so the need for spinal taps is no longer necessary. There are side effects, which include micro brain haemorrhages, but with monthly MRI scans, these are detected early and can be treated effectively. Most people have resumed their treatment once they have recovered.

Doctors agree that there are side effects, like any new drug. There were horrendous stories of lethal side effects with the AIDS drugs when they first came on the market, but now they are rare and have changed peoples' lives. The same is going to happen with these drugs and doctors are excited that finally there will be a drug which controls, or better yet, cures Alzheimer's and Dementia.

Dr. Sid O'Bryant, University of North Texas Professor and Executive Director, reminds us that, to date, medications to delay the progress of Alzheimer's have been ineffective because of the sub-types of this disease. Drugs that might work for one group of patients do not work for other groups. Alzheimer's is proving to be a different disease amongst different groups of people. The idea that one drug can successfully treat everyone is not working out.[14]

There are many factors with regards to Alzheimer's and Dementia, and no drug addresses all of those factors as of yet. Your Gerontologist may discuss the addition of drug therapy to try and slow the progress of Alzheimer's or Dementia, and with the advances being made daily, you will probably want to try any or all of them.

Marg had difficulty accepting this diagnosis in her once vibrant husband. This was not the retirement that they had planned, had worked towards. Carl frequently reminded her to never, ever send him to a Nursing Home facility. He made her promise to keep him and care for him at home. She promised to do so on one condition: That he never show violence toward her.

And tomorrow is another day...

CHAPTER 6

SUPPORTIVE CARE OPTIONS: AT HOME OR IN A FACILITY?

"I would rather die than be put in a home!"

How often have you heard that? And even though you are exhausted and lacking sleep, you assure your loved one that you will never place them in a Nursing Home. Now you are jeopardizing your own health.

When I first arranged for a caregiver to come and keep an eye on Charles so that I could have a break, she received a frosty reception. He told her that she was not needed and to leave immediately. Fortunately, she was an experienced caregiver and took it in her stride. Later when she tried to help with his jigsaw puzzle, he covered it up with his hands and would not allow her near it, just like a small child not wanting to share his toy. Many a time I would come home and find Charles in the dining room with his puzzle and the caregiver in the kitchen reading a magazine while keeping an eye on him from a distance.

Initially, Carl denied the need for Home Care and was adamant that he would have no part of it.

"Of course you are fine," I explained, *"but Home Care is there for your safety only. In the event of a fire while I was away, the Home Care worker would help you put your shoes on and get you to safety."*

"Home Care will be ok, but only for my shoes," he said.

Person-centred care, which focuses on caring for individuals diagnosed with Alzheimer's or Dementia at home, is at the heart of this book. It emphasizes treating the person with dignity and respect, taking into account their personal history, preferences and interests. By viewing situations from their perspective, providing opportunities for social interactions and encouraging engagement in enjoyable activities, you can enhance their well-being.

Furthermore, involving family, caregivers and the person with dementia (when possible) in developing a personalized care plan based on person-centred principles ensures a comprehensive and holistic approach to their care.

Alzheimer's and Dementia are becoming more common in the Indigenous communities, and we are aware that person-centered care is paramount in the Indigenous culture.

Dr. Kirsten Jacklin (www.i-caare.ca) and her team have published the following pictorials. The Medicine Wheel titled 'Preventing Dementia in Indigenous Peoples by Aging Well' was developed from advice from older Indigenous peoples.

PREVENTING DEMENTIA IN INDIGENOUS PEOPLES BY AGING WELL
Advice from older Indigenous peoples

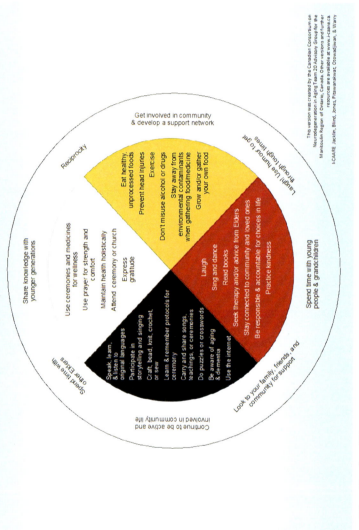

The 'Path of Dementia' can predict individual needs as the disease progresses.

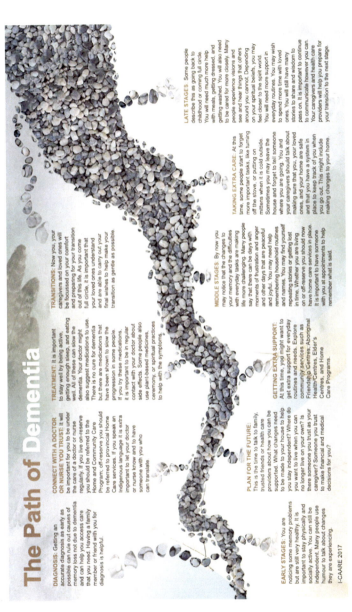

Reproduction of these images permitted as follows, (Dr Jacklin's team suggests the following citation for the factsheets): Jacklin K, Warry W, Blind M, Webkamigad S, Jones (2017) [Insert title of fact sheet] retrieved from: https://www.i-caare.ca/factsheets.

Everyone's journey is different

If you decide you cannot continue with the at-home care for any reason, and you must place a loved one in a facility, please be gentle with yourself. Be proud of the time you spent at home. You tried, and no one can ask any more. You can continue to be involved with your loved one's care and life while they are in a facility.

Tip: If you have to place your loved one in a facility, they will cling to you and beg you to "Take me home" when you go to leave. Your heart will feel like it is breaking and you will feel so guilty leaving them in tears. However, try to be inventive.

Someone I knew would tell his dad, "Oh no, not today, Dad. They are painting the house and you know how bad that smells. So you stay here one more day!" And his Dad would agree and calmly stay one more day. Every day was "one more day"! It worked and there was peace all around.

Home Care

Home Care is associated with, and funded by, the provincial medical care system. You can reach them through your health authority or health zone. Phone numbers are posted online as well. Your family doctor or Gerontologist can refer a client to Home Care and can give you their contact number.

The concept of Home Care is to keep the person living at home, and as independent as possible, for as long as possible, by providing care, support, assistance and equipment. In order to maximize independence, the client and family are taught to manage their own care with support from health professionals. The Home Care team usually consists of a nurse, social worker, physiotherapist, occupational therapist and care providers, depending on your needs.

In order to qualify for Home Care, a person must be assessed by a Home Care nurse (case manager). After the assessment, the case manager will inform you of the number of hours, (daily or weekly), that your loved one is qualified to receive. While in your home, the case manager will do a safety check and make suggestions and/or recommendations.

There is a cost associated with some equipment and supplies, such as raised toilet seats, tripod canes and walkers of various types. A commode chair might be needed, especially if the bathroom is a distance from the bedroom. Side rails for your loved one's bed may be suggested.

At some point, a hospital bed may be required. They can be rented from a medical supply store, the Canadian Red Cross or Aids to Daily Living. Check with your Home Care nurse for a referral. The supplying company will deliver and set up the bed. You may luck out and be given a bed on loan, but usually you will be charged a monthly rental fee.

These beds come with the mattress, full length side rails, a remote control to adjust the height of the bed and to raise the head and feet. You have to supply the mattress cover, linens and incontinence supplies. The Home Care nurse can supply you with these costs and will let you know exactly what duties the care workers are permitted to perform. They adhere strictly to this list of duties, so do not expect them to run a vacuum around the house or change a lightbulb for you.

The Home Care worker's main duties involve helping with the morning personal care, assisting with dressing, bedtime care, changing bed linens, and being present and monitoring someone for safety/security while you leave the house to run errands, go to appointments or to take a much-needed break.

A hospital-quality "pressure mattress" is a great idea. They can be rented from a medical supply company for $200 to $300 per month, and there are some systems for sale on the internet. The pressure inside the mattress constantly changes by way of an attached electrical pump, thus relieving continual pressure to the same area of the body. Some mattresses provide a vibration mode as well. We recommend an alternating pressure mattress, which is the type used in hospitals.

As the disease progresses, your needs may change. You may decide that you are unable to carry on and wish to check other levels of care. We touch lightly on some of these levels in order to help define them for you.

Designated Supportive Living is also known as Continuing Care. This type of care can be delivered in a facility or a care home where care aides are available twenty-four hours a day for monitoring and support. These accommodations will include meals and some health care supports at a cost depending on the facility chosen.

Long-Term Care, also known as a Nursing Home, is for someone who requires care which cannot be done at home. An RN, LPN or a Care Aide is available to deliver this care depending on individual needs.

Costs vary and are dependent on room type, (private or semi-private), and the level of care needed. Personal items like a telephone or TV and personal hygiene items are generally not included in the monthly cost.

In government-funded facilities, the cost can easily range from $1850 to $2250 per month, and it is considerably more in the private nursing homes. It is not always possible to place your loved one in the Nursing Home of your choice because beds are extremely limited in most areas. Often you are obligated to take the first bed which is offered to your loved one, even if it is at the opposite end of the city. You may then place your loved one's name on a waiting list for the nursing home of your preference and hope that a bed will become available quickly.

During my time as an insurance broker, I was sent to the US to train on long-term care insurance. I immediately saw the huge benefit it would have in later life and insisted that Charles and I purchase the coverage. Thank God we did because it enabled me to arrange for private home care and nursing home care for Charles (if we went that route). Unfortunately, not many people took my advice and now, of course, they regret it. Apparently, all the insurance companies have now taken this type of insurance off the market. If it is ever offered to you, I suggest you sign up for it immediately. It is not cheap, but it is more than worth it. It is akin to winning the lottery! One less thing to budget for or worry about in your retirement.

Your Home Care case manager may request your permission to consult Palliative Care or Hospice Care, depending on your loved one's needs.

Palliative Care is specialized care for someone with a serious illness. Care focus is on quality of life. There are no costs for personal care. There may, however, be fees or costs for equipment, supplies and some medications.

Hospice Care is for someone suffering from a serious illness for which there is no cure, and the doctor feels there is six months or less to live. The focus of Hospice Care is "comfort care" when facing the end of life. The provincial medical system covers the cost of the room and meals. There may be a cost or fee for specialized equipment and some medications.

Spiritual Care is available at both Palliative and Hospice Care.

It is best to call Home Care to get an assessment done as soon as possible. They are a valuable source of information, and they are there to give you a much-needed break. They are your support and your guide in caring for your loved one. Get the assessment done soon so that help is in place when you need it.

I found my case manager and care workers to be caring and gentle. Igwe showed compassion toward Carl during and following the daily linen change. He would remain at the bedside holding

Carl's hand and reassuring him that that repositioning was over and encouraging calm.

How to choose a Nursing Home

This is a checklist for the perfect Nursing Home.

If you have decided to pursue the Extended or Long-Term Care avenue, we suggest that you do your homework when you visit these places. Ideally, you should bring a family member or close friend with you because a second opinion is valuable. Do a drop-in or "surprise" visit a few days later with any additional questions. This way you can ensure that the first visit was real and not staged. Be aware of what the facility offers, what supplies they do NOT provide, and what the monthly costs are going to be. You will be surprised by how many extras are tagged on to the monthly bills.

1. Be aware of sights, sounds and smells when you are escorted through the facility during the visit. Consistent and unpleasant smells, buzzers ringing and not being responded to, or rudeness in overheard conversations between residents and staff, are not occurrences you want your loved to be exposed to.

2. Are there grab bars in the bathrooms? Are there railings in the hallways?

3. Is there enough staff to help the residents at mealtimes? What are the staff ratios to residents in the mornings and evenings, when they need assistance with personal care?

4. As the need arises, are there facilities available for an increased level of care? Are these facilities easily accessed or will your loved one have to be moved to a different building?

5. Costs: Is there an increased cost for the next level of care? If your loved one needs to be moved to a dementia unit, make sure that you visit that unit and begin the questioning process again.

6. When it is time to move into the unit, take pictures of your loved one's bedroom at home and try to replicate it in the new space. Bring the same pictures to hang on the wall, use their own furniture, and arrange clothes in the same drawers. These actions will make the surroundings more familiar to your loved one, and will help make them feel more settled and secure.

I went to visit three different Nursing Homes with my sons when I feared that I was reaching a point of utter exhaustion. People were beginning to voice their concerns about my health. They were all private homes ranging in price from $5,600 to $12,000 per month. In each one, we would have to provide the furniture. The rooms were nice, but we were concerned about the number of staff they had on the floor at night. Two or three staff members for forty-five to sixty residents, all with Dementia, and only hourly checks on them, was a concern for us especially with Charles' propensity to falling. We chose to keep him at home.

CHAPTER 7

THE DON'T CHAPTER

We are expecting some eye rolls here, together with "But it is so hard not to when they don't listen!" However, hear us out.

The Don't Chapter was developed from our experiences. You will soon be adding your own "Don'ts" as you move through this disease process.

Don't yell. They are not deaf, and yelling will increase their anxiety. They do not understand why you are angry with them. It may make them think they have done something wrong. They truly don't know what it could be, so it becomes frustrating for them. A person with dementia will not tolerate the strong tone and pitch of yelling or any other loud noises.

Don't argue. You cannot win an argument with a person who has Alzheimer's or Dementia. Arguing will increase the frustration and anxiety in both of you. A person with Dementia does not understand, so rather than argue, just change the subject and carry on. In the long run, does it really matter?

Don't ask if they remember. Of course, they don't remember—they have dementia. It is much easier to say, "Oh look, I found a picture of our children! It is so special," rather than saying, "Look at this picture, who are these people?" By asking if they remember, you could be reminding them that they don't remember, and that reminds them of their dementia diagnosis.

Again, does it really matter?

Why challenge the brain of someone with dementia? If you want to test their memory, you may want to begin the conversation by saying, "I remember when we were fishing with Cheryl and her husband. What was his name?" as you show them a picture of the fishing trip. This way you don't appear to be testing them.

Don't tell them that they are wrong. What good would come of telling them that they are wrong? Better to let them save face and maintain a shred of dignity. Learn to let it be. Let it go and encourage happy and peaceful behaviour. Letting it go will also decrease your stress and frustrations and will make it easier to laugh and think, *OK, whatever!* Try changing the subject and smile a lot. Ask your loved one to dance with you or give you a hug.

Do you want to be right or do you want peace and cooperation?

On occasion, I would drive to Caroline's home and visit with Charles while she took a much-needed break. I would help him work on his puzzle. Once in a while, I would place a puzzle piece in the correct spot and Charles' face would light up with a smile and he would say, "Jolly, well done!" He was such pleasant company and obviously easily impressed.

CHAPTER 8

THE LEGALITIES AND PAPERWORK

Many of you will have already taken care of these details, but we felt it was worth mentioning again. It is better to be prepared.

Advance directive is a document which your doctor or social worker can help your loved one complete, while they still have the capability of making their own decisions. This advance directive allows them to put their wishes regarding their care, and who they trust to make decisions for them, when they no longer can in writing.

Green sleeve is a green folder which contains a document indicating your loved one's wishes in the event of a cardiac arrest. This includes details such as, whether that person wishes to be resuscitated or have other extraordinary measures taken to keep them alive, (e.g., being placed on a ventilator). This form is completed by the physician. The entire folder MUST be kept on top of the client's fridge so that everyone in the healthcare industry knows where to find it.

Canada caregiver credit (CCC): You are allowed to claim $2350 under the Canada caregiver credit if you support a spouse or common law partner, but their net income must be less than $25,195. You may be able to claim an additional amount, up to a maximum of $7525, (according to income tax changes for 2022-2023). Check with a financial advisor or tax specialist. You could also get more information online at www.canadarevenueagency/caregiveramounts.

Power of attorney (POA) is a legal document identifying who can represent you financially when you can no longer make those decisions. This could be a relative, close friend or a lawyer.

Will: Make sure that a will is completed sooner rather than later. It is probably a good idea to involve a lawyer to ensure that the will and POA are legal; this can prevent issues down the road.

Bank accounts, etc. Ensure that bank accounts, safety deposit boxes and property, (including vehicles and real estate), are registered in both names in order to facilitate transfers later. This also applies to utility bills and other monthly household bills.

Accountant: Communicate with your accountant, especially if you or your loved one own a company or corporation.

CHAPTER 9

WHO WILL YOU CALL AFTER A DIAGNOSIS?

You may be in shock when you finally get the diagnosis. Normally you would discuss it with your loved one, but that is no longer possible as they don't know what is happening. We strongly recommend you choose a couple of close friends or family members who can support you.

I did not notify close friends until Carl was ready to do so himself. This was partly because I felt he had to accept and admit the diagnosis and partly out of respect for his privacy. Carl was encouraged to share his diagnosis, and he eventually did. Whether you choose to share this process with friends at the time of diagnosis or later, the decision is for you and your loved one.

Notify the immediate family because you will need help and support. Form a plan for your loved one's care needs, and organize days and times that work with family members so that you can get respite.

List the daily activities, meals, medications and personal care times for your loved one. Add your own needs and routines to this weekly schedule: hair appointments, doctor's visits, dental and eye care appointments are entered in the time slots.

Make your plan large enough to include your meal plan, and a sidebar could include the grocery list. A whiteboard is perfect for this task as you can colour-code events with different pens and, easily alter the plan as needed.

With this plan in place, you will quickly be able to schedule your respite breaks when friends or family call to visit. Offer detail and clarity in your plan so that relief caregivers can follow it. Suggestions on activities to keep your loved one occupied, such as playing cards, folding laundry, looking at photo albums, baking together, going to a park or chatting about a nature program on TV, are helpful. Remind every relief caregiver to observe your loved one closely and to never leave them alone. Safety issues and the possibility of wandering are always present.

Notify Home Care, (your specific home care number varies from town, to city, to province and can be found online; try typing "home care services for [your town or city]"), and request an appointment to have an assessment done. Get the ball rolling so that help is in place when you need it.

Notify the Alzheimer's Association locally. They are available to support, refer and answer questions nationwide. Call them anytime for advice and information on community programs and services. You may want to go online and search "Alzheimer's Association.ca." This site will bring up a section titled "Find your area's Alzheimer's Society," which lists the provincial phone numbers and websites for more information.

Notify friends because they need to understand the stress that you are under and can offer help, respite hours, or even just a short break. Friends can be your escape, your shoulder to lean on. Learn to accept help and make suggestions on how they can help. Friends are notorious for saying, "Call me if there is anything that I can do." If you have a list nearby with your needs itemized, you can get help immediately.

"Sure, my friend, I need to run errands later today, so can you come over and sit with him for twenty minutes?"

Or perhaps you could say:

"My house is a mess. I could really use about an hour of your help to vacuum, dust, change the sheets on the bed…"

Some friends may shy away from both of you, perhaps because they don't know what to say or do. Is it a fear of the unknown? A piece of advice for these friends: Help is time and time is help. The best thing you could do is give your time to sit and play cards with your friend or take them outdoors for a walk. Does the house need a little tidying up? Did you bring some home-baked muffins or a casserole for dinner? Walk a mile in your friend's shoes and the solutions to helping will be obvious.

Notify your neighbours as they can keep an eye out should wandering become an issue. Neighbours can also be that cheery face and smile when you are outdoors, and they are likely to be the first people you would run to should you need a safe place or a helping hand.

When I first told my sons of Carl's diagnosis, they were not surprised as the writing had been on the wall for a while. It felt like a heavy weight had just descended upon me and made breathing difficult. I felt numb, paralyzed. Now what?

CHAPTER 10

SAFETY FOR BOTH OF YOU

A diagnosis of Alzheimer's or Dementia does not mean they become weak overnight. In fact, they can become incredibly strong if they feel frightened and want to run away.

Many a time Charles would grab onto my hand or arm so tightly I thought it would break.

After he examined Carl, the Gerontologist advised me to set up a "run-away plan," in the event that violence reared its ugly head. (No, you cannot run away right now, although you probably feel like it!) We really understand that overwhelming feeling. Although I did not have to use the run-away plan, I did have it ready to implement.

A run-away plan: This plan is designed for the caregiver's safety and protection. In the event that your loved one threatens you, or you feel that an assault is imminent, your run-away plan should be initiated. Decide where you will run to. Make sure that your vehicle keys are handy. Do you have a coat or jacket ready at your exit? Remember that this is a grab-and-run situation and you have to plan and be organized enough to literally run out of the door. I wonder if this why Home Care workers wear indoor shoes in your home.

Avoid being trapped in a room, and always ensure that your quick escape through the doorway is possible. Position yourself so that you can be first out if need be.

Not everyone with Alzheimer's has an aggressive or violent tendency, but those who do can become angry in a quick moment; you need to be one step ahead.

Investing in a smart watch, a watch which is also a phone, GPS and computer, is a great idea. It allows you to run away without having to search for your phone to call for help.

You may want to hide a spare set of vehicle keys near your escape door, and make sure to keep your fuel tank at least half full. You may need that vehicle in the middle of the night, to keep you safe and warm while waiting for help to arrive.

It is best to call 911 if you feel threatened and describe your predicament to the operator. Give your loved one's history and a description of what made you feel threatened and caused you to run away. More information will be requested, as safety for you, your loved one and the responders is paramount.

The paramedics may show up to assess the situation and may decide to sedate the individual in the home, or bring them to the emergency department. Alternatively, the police may show up to ensure that you are safe, and they will take your loved one to the emergency department. Take direction from the response team as they see fit.

Guns and ammunition: Weapons need to be locked away or, preferably removed from your property. Even kitchen butcher knives should be removed from the easily-accessed block and placed in a drawer. Out of sight is out of mind. The same goes for scissors and other sharp objects. Just think of your own safety.

Tripping hazards: Home Care will remind you to walk through the house and remove tripping hazards, such as scatter mats that are easily moved, small step stools and ottomans that your loved one may have trouble noticing. You need to constantly be aware that your loved one no longer remembers that the ottoman is there, and could easily fall over it. Remember that their peripheral vision has probably deteriorated, so that ottoman or plant becomes a tripping hazard. Safe indoor shoes are recommended as opposed to floppy slippers, which may become a tripping hazard.

Falls: This generally starts in the middle stage of the disease when their balance becomes more unsteady. All seems to be fine when they are in motion, but when they stop to turn around or look backwards, they can easily fall.

Charles was always falling, especially while he was working in his beloved garden. Sometimes I didn't even know about the falls until he would present himself to me with a cut or cuts to clean up. He refused to believe that he had a balance problem.

"Look, I will prove it," he said one day, and he marched across the room swinging his arms. Then he did a sharp turn to come back and down he went! Fortunately, he fell into a dog bed, but it could

have been worse. He sheepishly admitted that his balance could do with some improvement!

Falls can cause a huge toll on caregivers.

Charles would often fall on his way to the bathroom in the middle of the night. He was not a big man, but 150 pounds of dead weight to get up off the floor on your own is like trying to move a mountain. My neck and shoulders have been badly damaged as a result, so please take care.

Tip: If your loved one has fallen and is on their back, try and get them to turn over and get into a kneeling position. Then place a sturdy chair next to them, or get them to hold onto the bed or a sofa and help pull themselves up.

Fall prevention: Introducing a cane or a walker is important at this stage. It takes a bit of persuading as they often feel that it makes them look weak. But keep trying as it really does help with the balance problem. Strategically placed grab bars throughout the house are helpful too.

My Home Care nurse suggested a side rail for our bed, not only for preventing a fall but also to provide assistance in getting out of bed. It was easy to install and could be lengthened when the need arose.

Charles was always eager to go upstairs to bed after dinner. Sitting in bed with his word find book was his favourite place to be. One night in his haste to go upstairs, he started climbing the stairs on his own. He missed his footing and fell backwards, landing on the tiled floor in the front hallway. He was badly injured and had to be taken to hospital by ambulance. This was the beginning of the end for him. Although we brought him home after two weeks in the hospital, he was never the same and ended up with two more admissions as a result of complications which followed that fall, before he died.

Tip: We suggest that you get a safety transfer belt, which are available at medical supply stores. These are strong, wide belts with adjustable closures and handles sewn into them. These handles allow you to assist your loved one with standing, sitting, balancing and even walking. Ensure that you are able and strong enough to handle the task before lifting them with a transfer belt. You must have a wide foot base and good balance otherwise you could fall with them—or worse still, end up underneath them.

Electric razors: These are a godsend as opposed to a blade. They do the job, they are safe, and it is OK if they shave ten times a day! They encourage self-care and independence, and they require minimal, if any, assistance. Sometimes they will even turn the razor on!

Stoves: They are a huge safety issue. You must check to ensure that the elements are off when cooking is complete. If possible, remove the knobs so that it is impossible to turn the stove on without you being present. At some point, you will take over the cooking tasks and assign your loved one to safer preparations like setting the table, pouring the water or sweeping the floor.

Ensure that your **smoke detectors** are functioning and the batteries are changed as recommended. A fire extinguisher kept handy in the kitchen area is advised. Familiarize yourself with the extinguisher, how to operate it and what type of fires to use it on. An ABC fire extinguisher will be safe to use on ordinary combustibles, flammable liquids, (like cooking oil), and electrical fires. This type of extinguisher is common and available at most hardware stores.

Medications: Place all medications in a secure or hard-to-access place. If medication is left out, you may have no idea how many pills, (if any), have been taken. A detailed paragraph on medications can be found in Chapter 17.

We had a pole installed in the ensuite bathroom. This helped Charles steady himself when stepping out of the shower or when he started to lose his balance. We also had grab bars installed next to the toilets around the house.

CHAPTER 11

WANDERING

One minute they are there and then, as if by magic, they are gone. It is just like caring for a toddler all over again.

When I had the POA for my friend, Annabelle, and I had to place her on a memory care unit, I discovered that wandering was quite a common occurrence there. The problem was that the residents would wander into each other's rooms and often take things which did not belong to them. I had read an article somewhere which recommended attaching big red foam hands to the door of each resident's room, with a stop sign in the centre. This seemed to cut down wandering considerably.

Sixty percent of people with dementia will wander away from their homes, and ninety-four percent of these wanderers are found within 1.5 miles from where they disappeared.[15] No one is sure what causes wandering; it could be multifactorial, and anything can trigger the brain to go for a walk.

Perhaps they are trying to get away from a loud noise.

If wandering occurs at about the same time of day, is it sundowning? Sundowning is associated with the increase in restlessness and anxiety at the time of day when the sun goes down, (more information in Chapter 15).

Were they told that they would soon be having a bath or shower and the fear of water sent them running?

Is something else scaring them or, did they have a hallucination?

If you are travelling, is the wandering occurring because they just want to go home?

Carl and I attended a family reunion at a large park. In a split second, he was gone! Panic, fear and worry overtook me. Where was he? There was a road nearby and it led outside of the park. There were geese all around, so there could be a body of water nearby as well. I felt sick to my stomach. I didn't want to think of possible outcomes, so we had to find him and quickly.

My sister, nieces and nephews hastily spread out in every direction calling for Carl. We came across a park attendant and obtained their assistance. Carl was found walking as if on a mission; he was not responding to calls of his name because he was focused on finding a washroom. We all breathed a sigh of relief and realized that, like a toddler, he could walk away quickly and quietly! I kept a close eye on him after that event.

Suggestions to help when wandering occurs:

Make a list of phone numbers, including your neighbours, family and friends to help you search.

Take a photo of your loved one every morning after they are dressed for the day. If you need to call the police because they have wandered, you will have a current picture and a description of the clothes they are wearing.

Ask your neighbours to call you if they see your loved one outside of the yard unescorted.

Marg had a security system installed in her home so that anytime a door was opened the speaker would let her know which door it was. It was a heads up, a warning. At night she would set the alarm to break-in and break-out mode. That alarm system brought her peace, security and greatly reduced her stress.

Alternatively, you could string four or five loud bells together and tie them securely to the doorknobs of all exterior doors. That way you will be alerted anytime the door opens or closes.

Global Positioning System (GPS) locators on neck chains are available through many companies. They can be life saving in the event of wandering, but only if the person with dementia is wearing it. They can easily discard anything that is not familiar to them. The same applies to a smart watch: It is only helpful if your loved one is wearing it.

A dementia bracelet, which is similar to a MedicAlert bracelet, can be engraved with your loved one's name, the caregiver's phone number and the word DEMENTIA or ALZHEIMER'S. This is a great idea because when you see an elderly person looking confused or lost, and you notice the MedicAlert bracelet, you automatically think, *'Ah, a medical condition!'* If you saw the word DEMENTIA, you would definitely not leave them alone. These bracelets apparently take two hands to undo and remove, so they are likely to remain in place.

Fortunately, we had Long-Term Care insurance for Charles, so I was able to hire private nursing care seven days a week. This meant that someone was with him all the time, so I did not have to worry about him wandering off on his own. Near the end, I had to hire someone to be with him throughout the night as well. Sadly, this type of insurance is no longer available in Canada.

CHAPTER 12

ELDER ABUSE

It is unfortunate that elder abuse is more common than is generally known. We cannot condone it in any way, shape or form, and we suggest that if you have reached a stage where your patience is gone, please ask for help.

Elder abuse is harm or distress caused to an elderly person, by someone in a position of trust. It can be physical, (including sexual abuse), emotional, neglect or financial in nature. The end of this section has websites and phone numbers for reporting elder abuse. A visit to their family doctor, if injuries are present, is in order and appropriate. The doctor will examine the senior and a paper trail is started, which will enable the physician to continue physical examinations and establish a reportable trend.

The elderly may be afraid to say anything about the abuse for fear of causing an escalation. Perhaps they are unable to describe these events because of their decreasing ability to communicate. People with dementia are much more vulnerable to being used or taken advantage of, and are often targeted.

Elder abuse can happen anywhere at home, in the community or in acute and long-term care facilities. It can be done by anyone, a spouse, a son or daughter, a caregiver, a friend or a staff member. Between four and ten percent of the elderly in Canada are affected by abuse, and only one case in five gets reported.

All abuse should be reported to your local police or call 911 if in immediate danger.

Types of elder abuse:

Physical abuse occurs when a caregiver or trusted individual inflicts physical pain or distress on an elder. This means applying physical force such as kicking, slapping, hitting, pushing and punching the person. Be observant, note bruises, scratches and cuts. Newly developed pain in extremities could indicate fractures. Note a new limp, weight loss and/or poor hygiene. Take pictures of the injury if possible.

Emotional abuse is unwanted behaviour that inflicts mental pain, fear or distress on an elder. It includes threats, humiliation, instilling fear, (including fear of violence), and insults to an elder. If this abuse is happening, you will notice a change in behaviour, fear of speaking and fear of expressing their emotions, especially in the presence of the offender.

Neglect is withholding basic necessities of life like water, food, shelter, hygiene and medical care. Make notes, document and report everything to the appropriate agency, doctor or the police if you suspect your loved one is being neglected.

Financial abuse is the improper use of an elder's money, assets or property for the benefit of someone else. It is done through stealing possessions and fraud. It can be committed by scammers or strangers as well as friends, caregivers and family. It can be difficult to detect until a pattern emerges. Look for recently opened bank accounts or new credit cards in the elderly person's name. Check the mail for letters from banks, for unexplained purchases, missing possessions and returned cheques with questionable signatures.

We have heard stories of elderly people being physically manhandled and pushed, as well as displaying unexplained bruises on their arms and legs. We've also heard stories of their belongings being stolen, especially jewelry and cash. There are people who will take advantage of our vulnerable seniors.

Be aware and be proactive. Perhaps placing valuable documents, jewelry and cash in a home safe would deter a crime. The special pieces of jewelry can still be worn and enjoyed as they are kept in a safe place in the senior's home. Perhaps leave a little cash in their wallet to impart a feeling of control of their finances.

Alzheimer.ca has many resources and more information on elder abuse.

The Canadian Network for the Prevention of Elder Abuse (**CNPEA**) website presents information and links to get help if someone you know is being abused or neglected. (xvi)

Here's a guide to services in Canada.

Province	Crisis Lines and Services
Alberta	Alberta Elder Awareness Council and Family Violence Information: 1-780-310-1818 (Multilingual service available) Seniors Abuse Helpline: 780-454-8888
British Columbia	Seniors Abuse and Information Line: 1-866-437-1940 Victim Link BC: 1-800-563-0808 (Bilingual service available) Domestic Abuse Crisis Line: 1-877-977-0007 Support Services for Older Adults Intake: 1-888-333-3121
Manitoba	Seniors Abuse Support Line: 1-888-896-7183 Domestic Abuse Crisis Line: 1-877-977-0007 Support Services for Older Adults Intake: 1-888-333-3121

Province	Crisis Lines and Services
New Brunswick	Chimo Helpline: 1-800-667-5005 Emergency Social Services: 1-800-442-9799 Beausejour Family Crisis Resource Centre: 506-533-9100 (Daytime); 506-312-1542 (Evening)
Newfoundland Labrador	Seniors NL Resource Centre: 1-800-563-5599
Northwest Territories	NWT Helpline: 1-800-661-0844 NWT Seniors Information Line: 1-800-661-0878
Nova Scotia	Neighbours, Friends and Families (Abuse and Violence Support Line): 1-855-225-0220 Adult Protection Services: 1-800-225-7225
Nunavut	Kamatsiaqut Nunavut Helpline: 1-800-265-3333 Elders Support Line: 1-866-684-5056

Province	Crisis Lines and Services
Ontario	Seniors Safety Line: 1-866-299-1011 Victim Support Line: 1-888-579-2888
Prince Edward Island	Island Helpline: 1-800-218-2885 Adult Protection Services: 902-368-4790
Quebec	La Ligne Aide Abus Aines (Elder Mistreatment Helpline): 1-888-489-2287 SOS Violence Conjugal: 1-800-363-9010 (Bilingual Service available)
Saskatchewan	Mobile Crisis Helpline: 306-757-0127 SK 24/7 Response and Crisis Lines: Prince Albert and area: 306-764-1011; Saskatoon and area: 306-933-620; Regina and area: 306-757-0127
Yukon	Abuse of Older Adults: 1-800-661-0408 extension 3946 Victim Link BC: 1-800-563-0808 (multilingual service available)

CHAPTER 13

A "WHAT IF" PLAN

While we see ourselves as strong and able to cope, we must prepare for the different eventualities...just in case.

What if you need surgery, suffer a fall and break your leg? You may require more than a few days of hospitalization, and once you are discharged to your home, you may not have the ability to care for your loved one by yourself.

What if you get cancer and need to go for chemotherapy? These treatments can be daily, five days a week and at times can produce nasty side effects. You may need someone to take care of you!

You must have a plan, a guide written down and ready to give to friends or family, in the event that you have an emergency. This plan will assist your relief or temporary caregiver, and maintain the routine and consistency of care for your loved one.

Your plan must include the following information on your loved one:

Family Doctor: name, office phone number and office address.

Health Care Number

List of Allergies

List of Medications: names, dosages and times of these medications.

Diet Preferences: likes and dislikes, amounts eaten in general and mealtimes. Snack suggestions for your loved one.

Daily Routines: time they awake in the morning, bedtime, mealtime, snack times. Morning and evening care and, if applicable, incontinence care. A list of suggestions for activities that your loved one can perform and enjoy would facilitate the transition.

Home Care Nurse: name and phone number.

Your plan could include a safety review for the new caregiver, that reminds them to lock doors, keep knives in the drawers and not displayed, and that medications must be kept out of sight in order to have control of them.

Also include tips on how to calm your loved one down in the event of escalating behaviour. Your absence will make them look for you, and suggestions for diversionary tactics will be appreciated. Perhaps their favourite television program will refocus them, and having the new caregiver sit with them to watch this program, will impart the feeling that they have not been abandoned and are not alone.

Notify your Home Care nurse of your upcoming absence from home, share your plan with the Home Care team and ensure that you are using the maximum number of hours of care aid that Home Care has allotted you. The relief caregiver will often be family or a friend and would not be expected to perform personal care. Therefore, requesting that Home Care workers do the morning and evening personal care and the changing of clothes, would be appreciated by the relief caregiver.

You may also need to rely on respite services until you get back on your feet. Respite is available at most Long-Term Care facilities, Nursing Homes and even small-town hospitals. Your Home Care nurse can assist you in locating respite services for a few days. There are also a few private facilities that charge for in-home respite care, or respite in their facilities. Charges and availability vary greatly, so planning ahead is advised, if possible.

Take all the time that you need to heal and strengthen yourself. This journey is difficult enough for a healthy caregiver.

CHAPTER 14

COPING WITH DEMENTIA BEHAVIOURS

By this stage of the disease, the brain is not reacting rationally. They become frightened easily and develop fears of certain things which make no sense. But to them it becomes a case of fight or flight.

Fears

Carl and I were going outside for a walk, so I was spraying his legs with mosquito repellant. You would have thought that I had sprayed acid on him as he screamed and yelled at me and kicked his legs! Do people with dementia develop an exaggerated response to sensations? Oh yes, sometimes!

Charles had a brain injury to his parietal lobe, (located at the top back part of the head), and the temporal lobe on the left side of his brain. He could no longer identify the sensation of hot or cold water touching his body, especially while being showered. He just knew that it was a terrifying experience for him. He would scream like a wild animal caught in a trap until the water was turned off. I dreaded shower days.

Agnosia

This is a condition which means hypersensitivity of all or some of the five senses—hearing, smell, taste, touch and vision. It can be a result of a stroke, dementia, developmental disorders or other neurological conditions where the occipital or parietal lobes of the brain are damaged.[16] There is no cure for this condition. It is a fight or flight reaction, (something that is still intact regardless of the Alzheimer's), so be aware that your loved one may lash out in self-defence.

They may develop a fear of water. Perhaps it is the shower head spray, maybe the temperature, or they are hypersensitive to anything touching them. Showers can become a difficult task, and perhaps the following suggestions will help you troubleshoot that fear. The only thing you can do is to gently explain what is going to happen and reassure them that it will be over soon.

Showering tip: Place a plastic lawn chair or stool, from a medical supply store, in the walk-in shower. Grab bars can also be installed in the shower to help them feel more secure, or the arm rests on the chair can help them stand up. Sitting makes them feel safer and it will prevent falls.

Start with tepid or lukewarm water and wet only their feet. Slowly and gradually increase the temperature to warm, and continue moving the shower head upwards. All the while, you are washing and rinsing because you do not know when the water tolerance will end.

If you have a standard bathtub and no walk-in shower, you might find that renting a long bath chair is helpful. Two of the chair's legs go in the bathtub and the other two legs are on the bathroom floor. These legs are adjustable and must be levelled and balanced before sitting on the chair. Your loved one then sits on a hand towel on the chair and slides in towards the tub. Meanwhile, you gently lift their first leg over the edge of the bathtub and inside. They keep sliding and you follow the same procedure with the second leg. Then your handheld shower can begin safely while they are in a sitting position in the tub. Coming out of the tub is a reversal of the procedure.

A handheld shower extension is reasonably priced at a hardware store and can be easily installed.

I tried wrapping a warm towel around Carl's shoulders, thinking that perhaps the chill of being naked was causing discomfort. It worked a few times but not consistently.

We tried everything we could think of to calm Charles while he was getting showered and also when he got out of the shower. This included warm towels and a fan heater blasting hot air into the bathroom, but he would howl and scream until he was fully dressed. There was simply no reasoning with him, so we tried to get it over and done with as quickly as humanly possible.

Tip: Please do NOT use the oven to warm a bath towel! There is too great a danger of a fire in the event that you forget the towel in the oven because you get distracted. And goodness knows how easily that can happen! Toss the towel or flannel sheet in the dryer for a few minutes. It comes out warm and cozy.

Tip: Please place a rubber bath mat on the floor of the shower as this will provide a bit of traction, and decrease the likelihood of a fall when they stand up.

You will reach a point where you can gauge a good day by whether or not you succeeded in the shower. *Wow, today is a great day! I managed to wash up to his armpits. YES!*

Anger and frustration

Just when you think that you are adjusting to this Alzheimer's, he does or says something to blow you away! I was getting ready to paint the bright blue walls in a spare room. Carl was watching me and he said, "So, how do you plan on removing the blue?" That was so difficult to answer because I realized how profound the disease had become.

Charles would get frustrated when he couldn't get the right words out. Sometimes he would clench his fists and hold his head but it was never anger directed at us.

Although a person may be diagnosed today with Alzheimer's, their symptoms will have started years before. Small changes in behaviour, emotion and memory have been occurring. Loved ones are noticing these changes and you should be documenting them, forming a timeline of occurrences. This timeline of events will be instrumental in diagnosing the disease when you return time and again to the doctor's office.

The subtle changes in personality and behaviour are not noticed by co-workers and friends, initially, because this individual attempts to hide and deny the dementia. They will avoid situations which may bring it forward, so they begin to isolate, to pull back and away from friends and society. They continue to work, drive and act like everything is normal.

As time goes by, more events occur, and family and friends gradually start to believe that something is wrong. By then the changes are pronounced enough that it is time to quit work, which brings about a huge change in personality and behaviour. Now the individual must admit to themselves, that their memory is failing them. Up until now they were able to deny it and continue working, driving and taking care of the house, but now they are caught. The gig is up, no more hiding. And trust us, they are very good at hiding this diagnosis.

There was a time when I wondered if I was going crazy! I would find myself lost, forgetting why I had entered a room, not sure what I was doing. I felt overwhelmed and had difficulty concentrating. My tears were always a small heartbreak away.

This admission that Alzheimer's has been diagnosed can uncover pent-up anger which can be displayed verbally or physically. Frustration of not being able to find the correct word or of no one understanding them, can sometimes lead to signs of violence, pushing you out of the way and clenching their fists.

For safety's sake, be hyper-aware of these behavioural changes. Pacing, heightened frustration, anxiety, tapping incessantly and forming fists, are all signs you need to watch for. Keep yourself safe and clear of physical assault. Keep your voice calm. Avoid high-pitched noises. No yelling. No loudness. You want to encourage a calm state in them. Remind them that you are here and you will help them to be understood. Take a few minutes to figure out what triggered this event, without asking too many questions. Asking a lot of questions can lead to more frustration and anxiety, and that leads to anger. So you must try to decipher the problem by troubleshooting. Where were they headed when this frustration occurred? What were they doing? What caused them to be troubled?

Give them space while encouraging calmness. Deep breathing for both of you will help. Once they have calmed a little, you will be able to gently guide them. Slide your hand into theirs and leave it there for a few moments without saying a word. Just a reassuring, "Shhh, quiet," will suffice, and soon you will notice that they are cupping your hand and slowly moving in your direction. The angry moment is over and you are able to redirect and hopefully resolve the initial issue.

Do not rush them. They need time to process the information, and your hand in theirs is the "information." Do not try to hurry them. Do not be pushy. Remain calm and gentle.

Personality changes are common in dementia, and these changes can occur without warning and at any time. Your loved one may display obsessive-compulsive behaviour early in the disease. They may lash out at you verbally, accuse you of untruths, swear at you, call you names, ask who you are and what the heck you are doing there. They may display behaviour that is very unusual for them!

Difficult? Yes, certainly.

It is time for you to take two deep breaths and tell yourself, *OK, whatever*. A quiet time out may help de-escalate the behaviour. Remain calm because your mood can be felt and transferred to your loved one. If you escalate your voice, tone or actions, they may follow suit. Play some soft music for them and place a book of pictures on their lap. If possible, take a few minutes by yourself and release your frustrations.

There was a power failure at home and, of course, the television did not work. I turned on the radio to divert Carl's attention and calm him. He became angry at me because the radio worked! I tried to explain that batteries were making the radio operational so a plug-in was not required. He called me on this, called me names. He said, "I don't know why you lie to me." It made me feel empty, drained. That heartbreak had arrived.

Repetitiveness

Repeatedly flushing the toilet became an issue at my home. Carl would just stand in the bathroom flushing the toilet, again and again. Rather than get angry, I forewarned him that, due to the wasting of water, and the cost of said water, I would be shutting off the water main and there would be no water for a while. My words were a waste of time because he was so enthralled with the flushing, that I don't think he heard me. I would ensure that the drinking water jug was full as well as the kettle, and then I would shut the water main off, while he was still flushing. He would then appear at my side to inform me that the water was not working!

"Yes, I see—perhaps it will return later," I'd say.

He was OK with that explanation and would walk back to the TV area.

Every day can bring a new issue. You must constantly be able to troubleshoot and problem-solve as calmly as possible. Remember to let it go, and take two deep breaths. This disease will test your patience. Incessant and loud tapping on the dashboard of your vehicle on a long drive will make you state, "Please stop tapping." The reply will be, "No, I like it!" And the tapping continues.

Tip: There are fidget aprons or lap quilts available online or, you can make your own in order to keep their fingers and hands busy. Fidget gadgets, (aprons, quilts and sleeves), were developed to elicit a sensory response in someone with dementia. They help bring about a calmness through touch. It may trigger a pleasant memory when touching a fuzzy or cozy patch of material. A fidget muff or sleeve can be made too. It could have a string of beads sewn on, a key, a zipper, a button and a loop of wool to go over the button. A shoebox containing a variety of safe items like cufflinks, bracelets, large beads strung on a string, small bottles with a screw top lid that can repeatedly be opened, loaded and unloaded will keep their idle hands busy.

When the same question is repeatedly asked all day long, although trying for the caregiver, it should be answered as calmly and pleasantly as when asked the first time.

The incessant noisy tapping or clapping their hands, for hours on end, might be redirected with a fidget item or by finding a tune that encourages tapping to a beat. If nothing else, there is always the option of turning up the volume a little.

Sometimes the repetitive behaviour will feel like it is driving you crazy, and you wonder how you will ever cope and manage for another day! You are normal. You need a break, so it's time to call on family or friends. Or maybe Home Care will arrive soon!

Focus on the strengths that you both have and try to maintain a positive attitude. Maybe go to the gym. It is refreshing to get out of the house. A little cardio workout will increase the blood supply and oxygen to the brain. And moving those joints will reduce stiffness, improve balance and decrease the incidence of falls.

Charles worked out with his personal trainer Kristian every week at his club and was incredibly strong as a result. He couldn't remember what he was supposed to do, but he followed instructions well. Not bad for ninety years of age! When going to the gym became too much for him, Kristian came to the house and continued the workouts until a few weeks before Charles died. He was a breath of fresh air for both of us.

Try brain stimulation exercises, puzzles, word searches, memory games. Play simple board games with the grandchildren. Watch nature shows on the television. Read the news headlines to your loved one as it might engage them in a conversation. The Alzheimer's Store Canada is an online site where you can look for ideas for games, activities and products. We are not endorsing this company, nor are we advertising for them. This is only a suggestion for ideas.

Charles was obsessed with jigsaw puzzles, and the harder they were, the more he liked them. He would spend hours focusing on them, oblivious to what else was going on around him. As the disease progressed, we could visibly see the state of his brain by watching how long it would take him to complete these puzzles. As his skill diminished, we reduced the size and complexity of the puzzles.

He also loved word find books, especially when he was lying in bed in our bedroom. I have a lovely photo of him sitting up in his hospital bed the day after his horrendous fall down the stairs with his word find book and pen in hand. The sad part was that the book was upside down and his poor damaged brain had not figured that out yet.

Go for walks together, (if your loved one is still mobile), and enjoy the seasons. Do some deep breathing while walking. Enjoy the senses, the sounds...birds singing. Enjoy this very moment. As someone once said, "Stop and smell the roses."

Encourage them to help with household chores, folding laundry, setting or clearing the table, drying dishes, sweeping the kitchen floor, (who really cares if you have to sweep it again later), raking leaves, sweeping the driveway or garage floor, cleaning the vehicle.

He still needed supervision. One day Carl decided to help me by cleaning the mat at the back door. He got the hose and spray nozzle ready and did a wonderful job of cleaning the mat. Next time, I hope he will take the mat outside first! There was water all over the entry, floor, stairwell, walls and shoes.

Maintaining a positive attitude

Today was the best day ever! Carl told me that I was the most beautiful young lady that he ever saw and that he loved me very much. A short moment but everlasting in my heart.

Work consistently at maintaining smiles and laughter, and turn issues and problems into fun. This will decrease anxiety and increase cooperation. The more you smile, the less stress is upon you.

One day, I took our puppy for a short walk and upon returning I found every door in the house wide open...it was winter in the prairies! I said to Carl, "Goodness, who opened all the doors?" He replied, "Oh, not me." I smiled, laughed and said, "Must be those ghosts!" He laughed as well and said, "Yep, ghosts." The moment was over, no harm done. Everyone was happy, which sure beats angry.

People with Alzheimer's see their own beauty, and they force us to slow down as we are so busy and always in a rush. During Carl's last Christmas season, he appreciated our neighbour's light display. Every time he would look out the window he would say, "Oh my God, look at how beautiful that is!" And five minutes later, he would enjoy that display of lights again and repeat the same line. When I thanked the neighbour for the display and explained what was happening at my home, he put up even more lights! Carl was thrilled! Thank you, Dana. You made his last Christmas so special.

While in Medicine Hat, I took a short online course in quantum physics and I would call Carl over to see the pictures on the computer. He always hurried to see these pictures because he loved the bright colours, the shapes and the crystal-like images against the black background of space. He was almost mesmerized. I am glad to have the memories of each smile.

Charles saw beauty in our two dogs and remembered their names throughout his journey, even when he had forgotten who we were. He wanted to know where they were every minute of the day. Upon discharge from the hospital after his bad fall, we arranged for a hospital bed to be put in the sitting room. This allowed him to watch the neighbours drive by and he would comment on how nice it was to see the snow on the rooftops of all the houses! The dogs used to hop up on the sofa in front of his bed so he could talk to them. They were happy to have him home again!

Every person will see their own beauty. Cherish that memory.

CHAPTER 15

SUNDOWNING

What is going on here? He did the same thing yesterday and the day before. What is happening? Why is he so restless and agitated?

Welcome to sundowning.

Between 4:30 and 5:00 in the afternoon, Carl became increasingly agitated and anxious. He paced more, was angrier and more argumentative. I could clearly see the increase in his frustrations. He would open all of the exterior doors and leave them wide open, regardless of the weather and temperatures. He was restless and unable to sit for a meal; he'd get up, pace and return for another bite of dinner. Conversation was impossible as he could not find the correct words. He seemed more lost than usual.

Sundowning is often referred to as "late day confusion," and it generally happens between 3 and 8 p.m. It usually begins during the moderate stage of dementia and affects approximately sixty percent of people with Alzheimer's disease and other types of dementia. It can cause confusion, aggression, anxiety, pacing, wandering and not wanting to follow any directions. Paranoia and hallucinations may also take place.

The true cause of sundowning has yet to be discovered, but it is believed to be due to the disruption of the normal circadian rhythm, (the body clock). This could happen because of a lack of sleep, being in unfamiliar surroundings, low lighting which may cause shadows, sadness, depression, tiredness, pain and yelling.

Before diagnosing sundowning, you must rule out an infection, (a urinary tract infection or a chest infection). Take their temperature and heart rate and check if they are making frequent bathroom visits. Are they coughing? Report the presence of these symptoms to your doctor and follow the treatment prescribed.

If there is no infectious process happening, you may recognize the same things happening every day. Now you will begin to anticipate "the witching hour" as the sun goes down.

How to decrease the severity of sundowning

Follow the same routine every day. Introducing a change in the daily routine can create anxiety in an individual with Alzheimer's. Adhering to your dinner and bedtime routines may help maintain calm.

When Caroline was working in London, UK, she would sometimes take extra night shifts at a nursing home nearby. Every evening when she came on duty, she would find all these ladies walking around with aprons on, and dusters in their hands. Some enterprising staff member had the brilliant idea to give them a job to do and it really seemed to calm them down. It also helped the housekeeping staff!

Make sure that they get lots of natural light every day. It may be worth trying a sunshine lamp, (available at such stores as Canadian Tire or Amazon). Perhaps moving their favourite chair near a window facing West, will get them a little of the afternoon sun, shining brightly. Exposure to sunlight has been proven to be successful for many people with dementia.

Marg tried the sunshine lamp, leaving it to shine over Carl for hours. Unfortunately, it did not seem to have any effect.

Try to avoid naps when possible. That may be difficult as those naps are your own precious breaks.

Create a calm space in the room by playing familiar music or nature sounds. Try to organize your day to be able to sit with them when sundowning begins. They may calm more readily with your presence, and it will help decrease their fears and tension.

Reduce stimulating background noise. Try shutting the sound off on your phone, in an effort to maintain a calm moment.

Offer a snack or suggest an activity.

Being together reinforces the feeling that they are safe, that you care and will help.

As with all situations in dementia, avoid arguing or restraining them as this will increase their agitation.

Use nightlights in the bedroom.

If your loved one demonstrates anger during this time, you must inform the doctor and get medication to help with the problem. Verbal anger is common during the sundowning hours, and physical anger occurs in about thirty percent of people with dementia.

During Carl's sundowning phase, he once became agitated, frustrated and he placed his hands on my shoulders and angrily pushed me away. I was very scared. I feared that that he might escalate this behaviour. I made myself as large as possible by squaring and lifting my shoulders. I raised my arms and in a loud voice said, "Stop!" I then reminded him that if he hurt me, he would go to a Nursing Home. This was not a threat, it was a promise. He backed away from me and redirected himself to the television area.

CHAPTER 16

THE POWER OF MUSIC

"If music be the food of love, play on!" - **William Shakespeare**

Music has long been known to help humans and animals.

One large boarding kennel where I housed my dogs while we were on vacation played the pan pipes (Zamfir) into the kennel area and the dogs immediately settled down. They also loved Nana Mouskouri. Who knows why?

Social worker Dan Cohen set up a program to bring iPod and music therapy to nursing homes across the USA.

Filmmaker Michael Rossato-Bennett chronicled the astonishing experiences of individuals who have been revitalized through simply listening to music. *Alive Inside,* (available on YouTube), is truly amazing and heart-warming to watch. The camera reveals the uniquely human connection we find in music and how its healing power can triumph where the prescription medications fall short. They discovered that the parts of the brain which remember music are not affected too much by Alzheimer's or dementia. Thanks to Functional Magnetic Resonance Imaging (FMRI) machines you can actually see those parts of the brain light up when people listen to their favourite music.

During the filming of this documentary, they introduced us to many patients with advanced stage dementia, some who had withdrawn so deeply from society that they had not responded in any way to their caregivers or family members for a long time. By way of interviews with these patients' families, Michael and his team found out about their backgrounds, what they liked to do when they were younger, and more specifically, the types of music they liked to listen to in the past. Armed with this knowledge, they downloaded personalized music menus onto little MP3 players, attached headphones to them and placed them on the patients' heads. The results were remarkable. Bear in mind, some of these patients had been lying in a fetal position for months and sometimes for years. As they listened to the music, their feet started tapping to the rhythms. Some patients lifted their heads and smiled, while others started to sing the words.

Even more amazing was how, in some cases, patients who had been so withdrawn in the dark and lonely world of Alzheimer's, started to talk to their caregivers and family members about their memories and were perfectly lucid for long periods afterwards! Music succeeded where medicine had failed.

Perhaps playing music for your loved one who is at the beginning, middle or end of their journey is something that could help them. What have you got to lose? Make a note of their favourite songs, artists or composers and download them onto a little MP3 player. They are inexpensive and available from places like Best Buy and Walmart. Just imagine, you could help soothe your loved one when they are confused, anxious or withdrawn just by playing music. And maybe they could carry on a normal conversation with you again, if only for a little while.

Tip: Make sure that they listen to the music through the headphones. Apparently, it makes a significant difference because it blocks out all outside noise.

CHAPTER 17

TROUBLESHOOTING

When you are at your wits' end and nothing seems to calm your loved one, this is the chapter for you. We will focus on problem-solving and how to read your loved one's behaviour. They may be unable to effectively communicate their needs, so you have become their interpreter.

Walking and balance

What if your loved one does not want to walk anymore? Are their shoes on the correct feet? (This common reality can also be a real tripping hazard). Maybe there is a pebble in their shoe that causes pain, so they don't want to walk.

If you notice a change in their gait, they begin to shuffle their feet and take very small steps, you must watch their balance. Will a walker or cane help? You will need to be more vigilant about tripping hazards around the house.

Restlessness

They are pacing and have increased anxiety but cannot explain why. Are they having tummy cramps because they need to have a bowel movement? The tummy says that a bowel movement is about to happen, but the brain does not recognize the urge, and does not tell the body to go to the bathroom. With your guiding hand, lead your loved one to the bathroom and ask them to sit there for a few minutes.

Encourage your loved one to expend some of that restless energy by increasing their physical activity. Go for a walk outdoors, sweep the walkway, do a few minutes of chair exercises, or provide them with a fidget lap quilt.

If they are wandering, maybe hiding their shoes will help. Replace the shoes with something to distract them and redirect their attention. For example, a box of pictures from their youth, their interests and their life.

Decreased appetite

Your loved one says, "I am not hungry," and pushes away an untouched plate of food, so something is wrong. Maybe the concept of using a knife and fork to cut the food is too difficult for them. Perhaps they cannot figure it out and it has become overwhelming. Try dicing the meat and mashing the potatoes, for example, and put the plate in front of them again. More than likely, it will be happily devoured. If all your loved one wants to eat is ground foods or soft foods, try chopping the food and, of course, add gravies and sauces to make everything easier to swallow.

Tip: Avoiding patterned plates is recommended because the pattern gets mixed up with the food. This can cause difficulty when trying to differentiate between the pattern and the food. Because of their diminishing vision, the solid-coloured plate will highlight the food portions.

Sooner or later they will start using their fingers to pick up the food. Allow this to happen because it gives them a modicum of independence to feed themselves.

Be observant of "chipmunk cheeks"! This occurs when they repetitively add food into their mouth without chewing or swallowing. Did they forget to chew or swallow? Perhaps either one, and they are in danger of choking on chunks of food. Gently remind them to chew and swallow.

At one point, Carl would go to the bathroom and spit out the food that he had stored in his cheeks. Then he would push the food bits down the drain. He said, "Look, this stupid sink is broken," after the drain had plugged. I was astounded at the amount of food he had packed in that drain.

As the disease progresses, changes in appetite and the inability to use utensils will lead you to assist with feeding. Initially, simply guide their hand and let them hold the utensil. As their needs change, ensure you change with them; you will need to get used to the idea of feeding them.

There will be a time when they will refuse to drink, and may not even take a few sips of water throughout the day. Encourage their favourite drinks, even if they contain sugar. People with dementia and Alzheimer's crave sugar. At this point, does it really matter? Which is worse: no fluids or fluids with sugar?

Carl usually took his coffee black and now he was refusing it altogether. I began adding cream and sugar, and I did not use the word "coffee" when I brought it. He enjoyed it and frequently requested a second cup. Overall, his fluid intake improved.

Choking

This can become a serious problem as the dementia advances. It is recommended that thicker fluids should be offered to prevent with this hazard. There are thickening agents, which can be purchased at the drug stores, to add to their regular drinks if necessary. It is also advised to not have them drink through a straw as this can also cause choking.

Administering medications

There are a few ways to get your loved one to take medications.

You can crush the pills and mix the powder in yogurt or pudding. The medications that cannot be crushed can be hidden in lumpy food like oatmeal, mashed potatoes or even soup. There will come a time when your medication tricks won't work. At that point you may wish to discuss this problem with the doctor.

Perhaps the medications need revision? Are some of them available in liquid form?

Tip: Your pharmacist can blister pack pills, meaning that the pills are packaged in a soft plastic bubble for a particular time of day and cover seven days of the week; each day is identified so you are aware of the medications taken. BUT before you run out and do this, please check into the cost. Some pharmacies say they do not charge for blister packing, but they will dispense only a one-month supply of your pills. Then, the next month you get charged another dispensing fee. For example, if you typically spend $50 for a three-month supply of pills, the pharmacy may charge you $50 per month to have these pills blister packed! That means you will pay $600 a year for the same pills that used to cost $200.

Consider buying a few dosettes, which are reusable plastic containers divided into 7- or 14-day compartments, each with a snap closing lid. Purchase different colours for different times of day and load them yourself. If you are not able to do that, consider having a family member help. Whether you do blister packs or dosettes, remember that neither is childproof, so keep them out of sight and secure.

Help with getting dressed

Distant supervision while your loved one is getting dressed is advised. We say distant because you want to encourage independence for as long as possible. However, sometimes it is difficult to get your legs into the sleeves of your sweatshirt, and at times you need to remind them that underwear goes on before the pants. A gentle guiding hand, smiles and patience all work well.

Having a chair near the bed was helpful as it was a visual clue for Carl to sit down to put his socks or pants on. To him, the bed was a place to lie down. This was very effective. I positioned it near the night table thereby allowing Carl to lean on the table to help him stand. It helped him maintain his balance and it saved my back.

Belts, buttons and zippers were becoming difficult for Carl, so jogging pants were the solution and became a forever part his wardrobe. I could rest assured that he was presentable whenever we went out.

CHAPTER 18

GETTING OUT AND ABOUT

They say "A change is as good as a rest," so why not go out for a car ride?

Unfortunately, Charles did not enjoy his journey. It reminded me of taking the kids on a trip and the chorus of "Are we there yet?" being chanted from the back seat. But now it was coming from a super-agitated husband! We did not try that again except for medical appointments.

Carl tried to convince me that I did not have to stop at a STOP sign.

"That means Go!"

"Yes, Dear. I see why they pulled your license!"

I received a call one afternoon from the Calgary Police Department asking if anyone in our house drove a red truck. It turned out that Charles had cut a driver off while changing lanes and was completely oblivious to it. Of course, it had to be a high-end vehicle which ended up costing $6000 in repairs! When Charles arrived home, I met him in the garage and showed him the damage to the *side of his vehicle. He was shocked and frightened that his license would be taken away immediately. Two more minor accidents in the following three months meant it was time for him to hand over his keys. I know how hard it was for him, but he accepted that it was best for everyone's safety—and our budget!*

As if the diagnosis itself is not bad enough, your loved one will likely lose their driver's license. The item that brought them freedom, independence, excitement and made them feel mature all those years ago has been taken away. They are now told that they are not good enough to drive. Wouldn't that make anyone angry and frustrated?

It is your responsibility to discuss their driving behaviour with the doctor and report inappropriate speeding, unsafe lane changes, getting lost, not obeying traffic signs or road rage. The doctor will then pull the driver's license and report it to the Department of Motor Vehicles (DMV) resulting in you receiving a letter requesting they surrender their license. Keys to the vehicle must be put away to prevent unauthorized use. As you'll likely take over the driving, be prepared for constant critiques as it may be their way of coping.

Grocery shopping can still be a treat. It gets you both out of the house and becomes a bit of a social event. As long as you are not in a rush, they will probably enjoy pushing the cart and meandering through the store with you. Pushing the cart also reassures you that they have something to hang on to for balance.

One day a customer in the grocery store had left a cart in the middle of the aisle, and this cart was in Carl's way... Carl became instantly angry, shoving the cart out of his path and forcing it to crash in the display shelves. After apologies and short explanations, we decided that it would be best to go shopping at quieter times of the day.

I wish that I could have somehow let the world know what Carl was going through, in the hope that strangers would have had more patience with him as he crossed the street, or manoeuvered a grocery cart in the parking lot.

Travel can certainly still be done as long as you are aware that all reservations, flights and scheduling will be your responsibility. Remain observant and don't take anything for granted, no assumptions.

For example, the elevators may be overwhelming...so many buttons. How does this work? Yikes, which button do I press? Which room is ours? What floor is it on?

Then the restaurants. Which restaurant? A menu? More decisions...it is OK. Remain calm. You choose the restaurant and the dishes—after all, you know their likes and dislikes, so make it work.

One day they might say, "I just want to go home. I miss my chair." And you will know that travelling is over.

I was not brave enough to travel with Charles after the dementia diagnosis. To be fair, he did not enjoy travelling and I had no reason to believe that would miraculously change. He was much happier in his home and his garden.

While in our hotel in Mexico, Carl and I would play a game. We would race each other, from the main floor, to see who would arrive at our room door first. Carl would take the elevator and I would race up the two flights of stairs. Usually it was fun for both of us, but the last time neither of us won the race. Carl had not arrived at our room. I had to go back to the main floor and found him in the elevator, staring at the panel of buttons and not knowing what to do. He had forgotten what floor our room was on and did not remember how to operate the elevator.

I realized then that our travelling days were over. It had become stressful and I found myself constantly on edge, unable to relax or enjoy the locale. I realized that Carl would be happier to stay home, and it would be much easier for me as well.

CHAPTER 19

INTRODUCING COMMUNITY ACTIVITIES

Desperation starts to come in waves, just like the feeling of being trapped in the house with no end in sight. We know that you are stoic and can cope on your own, but you are beginning to feel somewhat overwhelmed and exhausted.

It is time to get help.

Our boys thought that it might be a good idea for Charles to join the Canadian Legion. They felt that meeting former soldiers might give him a place to go and meet like-minded people. Sadly, it did not work. I think he was already embarrassed by his failing speech and so he became even more withdrawn when we went there.

Carl tried two different day programs. I stayed right by his side on both of those occasions. He did not appear fearful or anxious, more like disinterested and bored. After being there for four hours, he walked out of the front door, with me chasing after him. I encouraged him to return, but he remained resolute in his decision.

"I am not crazy," he said.

Once requested, the Home Care nurse will book an appointment to assess your loved one. This assessment will take two to three hours to complete and includes, a detailed past and present history of your loved one and, a walk-through of your home identifying and making recommendations regarding safety issues.

You may want to look into Adult Day Programs, often operated by church groups or hospitals. Some Long-Term Care facilities offer a similar plan, but these have been curtailed since the onset of COVID-19. Good Samaritan centres offer programs with socialization, a little exercise, (nothing extravagant), and a little mental stimulation, (discussions on current events globally as well as locally). The program generally lasts four hours and includes coffee and lunch. The fee is usually enough to cover the costs, and you also sometimes get to choose which days of the week work best for you.

The sooner you start this Day Care program the better because, structure and routine are so important in the Alzheimer's life. An early start and sticking with it, will help them accept the plan. Accompany them initially to help ease them into the program, and keep reassuring them that you will return to bring them home.

Community Seniors' Groups usually have scheduled hours where you can drop in for selected activities. They may offer puzzles, card games, chair exercises or perhaps a cup of tea to round off your walk. You can find your local groups by searching "seniors community groups" online.

Meals on Wheels is a non-profit organization that allows you to choose which meal(s) and which days you require the meals delivered to your home. To be eligible for a reduced cost you must provide the previous year's income tax Notice of Assessment. In Calgary, you may try a Dinner Sampler, which gives you a choice of four meals delivered to your home for $25. For more information, go to 'www.mealsonwheels.com'

Contact your local Alzheimer's Association for information on local programs and Societies that help with the needs and concerns of people experiencing Alzheimer's and their caregivers. Church groups often offer assistance with someone in need, whether it be support and friendship for you, the caregiver, or time sitting with your loved one supplying safety and security, while you take a break.

When the disease progresses and you are unable to leave them alone for even one minute, create a schedule for family or friends to relieve you of responsibility, as often as possible. You will need the break to breathe deeply, to meditate or to just get away.

Every day, Carl enjoyed a bowl of soup for lunch. It had to be accompanied by eight buttered crackers—not seven and not nine. He would line them up and count them. One day while our son Brian, was watching over his father, he had served the soup and crackers for Carl's lunch. Carl ate more crackers than soup and Brian said, "Well, I kept buttering the crackers and he kept eating them, so I would butter more. He did not count them today!" I enjoyed the break and I believe that Carl enjoyed Brian's visit.

CHAPTER 20

CAREGIVER CARE

When you are in the middle of this journey, you enter a coping mode. You fool yourself into believing that everything is under control, but others notice your exhaustion, your weight loss, your refusal to go out for lunch or dinner, because you cannot leave your loved one. The signs are there: It is time to start looking after yourself.

Caring for a loved one with dementia will be challenging, stressful, trying, exhausting, draining and seem endless. It will also have moments of laughter, humour and undying love. This promise is difficult and requires love, attention, care and patience.

But you must look after yourself; you cannot afford to be sick now.

In your role as caregiver you will need:

Sleep: Adequate sleep is necessary for you to continue with your daily routine. Sleep will strengthen your resolve and grant you some patience and gentleness to get you through each day. Your loved one will wake you multiple times during the night, so you will need the opportunity to get a good sleep. Ask for help. Perhaps a family member could relieve you of your responsibilities for a few hours so you can sleep.

Respite care: Check with the local Long Term Care facilities for availability of respite beds. Respite beds are booked ahead of time. They provide total care of the individual and can usually be booked for two or three day durations. Respite bed information, phone numbers and costs are available through your home care nurse.

Some agencies offer at-home respite, which allows you to walk away for a number of hours or the entire day. They normally charge by the hour, and costs vary.

A balanced diet: As you know, food is your energy and it keeps your immune system strong. Accept dishes from family, friends and neighbours. Ask for help with meal preparations if you need it. Make freezer-friendly meals and enjoy the convenience of that later. Perhaps there is a Meals on Wheels available in your community that could help for a few days of the week.

Exercise: Try to make time for a few minutes of cardio. Ride a bike, use a rowing machine, do a gym workout or a dance class. Exercise will rejuvenate you and your outlook will improve. You will have a feeling of accomplishment and satisfaction, it is also energizing.

Breaks: You need a break. Take advantage of every fifteen-minute break offered. A "walk away" break will relax you. Deep breathe as you walk away, be present with your surroundings, hear the birds, smell that fresh air, feel your shoulders drop and your tension melt away. You will return, (and yes, you must return), refreshed and ready to complete your day! Home Care help, family or friends can be asked to stay for fifteen minutes while you walk away.

Mental and emotional health: Sometimes a visit from friends is not possible, (remember the COVID-19 restrictions?), so on those occasions try calling a friend. Unload your frustrations, connect with the outside world, share your day and laugh. And then laugh again. Laughter releases endorphins, those feel-good hormones which relieve stress, increase your oxygen levels and stimulate your immune system.

I called Caroline every evening after settling my husband for the night. Some calls were short because she was caring for Charles, and some calls lasted forty minutes. We would share our days and inevitably would laugh. I would always feel an Ahh, what a relief moment and life was good again.

I would spend twelve- to fourteen-hour days by Charles's bedside in the hospital. There were COVID-19 outbreaks everywhere, so we could not leave his room. Some days were more exhausting and worrying than others. Every night on my way home, I would call Marg and unload all my concerns and frustrations on her. She was so good about letting me vent and would then offer suggestions to help with the problems. I will never forget her incredible friendship and support.

Keep a diary: You will be exhausted and will not remember every detail of your journey, so jotting a note will be your reminder later when you can do a transcription. Document the changes, events, challenges and emotions you are experiencing, such as continuation of the timeline changes that you documented before and during the time of diagnosis. Keep writing.

I found that documenting my journey in caring for my husband was rewarding. It made the experience OK, and it felt like I was unloading to a friend. Later, these notes proved valuable in reassuring me that the right decisions had been made.

Your safety: As previously mentioned, have your escape or run-away plan in place. Ensure that items that could be used as weapons are locked away.

Support groups: As a caregiver, you will need support and reassurance because you may not want to lean on friends and family all the time. Support groups are great because they allow you to share information, unload feelings and help you feel that you are not alone. Tips and tricks in care and management are shared.

Did I find a stream of tears quietly flooding my face at night before succumbing to sleep? Yes, of course. And were these tears because I felt sorry for myself? Yes! And were they because I was exhausted? Definitely!

Take care of yourself: Be gentle with yourself; it is OK to cry. Crying is a release of those pent-up emotions.

Your loved one is not alone on this journey because you are there, feeling every moment. This experience, with all of its emotions and feelings, is yours too. No one can judge you, no one should tell you what or how to feel. Whatever you feel is right at that moment. You are allowed to feel, to cry and to get frustrated and angry. Slam your fists in a pillow or really scrub that floor and release your anger without escalating around your partner.

I recall getting rather upset with people who said, "God only gives you as much as you can handle," or "When God closes a door, He opens a window." Jails probably do that too—and I felt like I was in one! Another one was, "You are lucky because you are a nurse." Really? I sure don't feel very lucky! Remember to just "let it go"!

CHAPTER 21

THE SANDWICH GENERATION

Vacienne, our granddaughter, would help Charles play cards or memory games. She would give him clues or guide his hand to the card he needed to play. It was very sweet to witness the relationship between them.

This is now becoming a fairly common situation with women having babies later in life, and then being required to help with aging parents at the same time. The stress of trying to care for both, and sometimes having to work full-time, can be exhausting.

There are people who live in multigenerational homes, so the idea of having a grandparent around is normal for them. But for the bulk of us, it is a huge adjustment. We are getting married later in life, having our children at a later age, and are having fewer children than previous generations, which means there is less help to share the load later in life.

Some of us are caught in the "sandwich generation" where we have to care for an elderly parent with dementia, while trying to raise our own kids, keep our job, maintain our social circle and drive children to sports events and school programs. And we are also expected to make time for our spouse, possibly make meals and contribute to the housework and yard work. It feels never-ending. Some of us are wound up tighter than a drum and are running short of patience.

BREATHE four times—deep and slow breaths. Get the oxygen to your brain so that you can clear your mind and make good decisions.

Ways to integrate a loved one with dementia into the home

1. Before you can expect a child, (no matter what age), to cooperate and help, you must explain, describe and educate them on what Alzheimer's disease is, and how it affects the brain. Talk about the changes in mood, movement, speech and emotions, which have become the new normal with their grandparent. Be honest and help your child understand that frequent repetition will be necessary, and that loud noises will offend and upset their grandparent. Remind them that loud noises will be allowed but in a different locale, perhaps outdoors or in the garage or basement of the house. You are not stopping them from being kids and having friends over, just designating what areas are off limits for noise.

2. Call a family meeting and let everyone have a say. Involve the kids in the care of their grandparent. A fourteen-year-old can help watch a grandparent after school, keeping them safe while waiting for you to get

home from work. A six-year-old can help clear the table for Grandpa, then play a game of Go Fish and even bring him a glass of juice. Help kids feel like they are part of the family plan in caring for their grandparent with respect, love and especially laughter.

3. If the kids are part of the decision-making process and are involved with the caring, they will accept the family commitment, and they will help. Kids know more than you realize. The more open you are, the better the communication will be, and the more supported the child will feel.

4. Accept help. Home care, friends, family, neighbours—accept help from anyone and everyone. Help with housework, yard work and especially with respite. You will need a few hours to regroup and be that special family.

5. When you are out and about running errands, try to bring your loved one who has dementia with you as much as possible. It may take a bit longer to get everything done, but the benefits of sleeping better and socialization for them is worth it.

6. Make mealtime a true family time with duties for everyone. That way everyone can watch Grandpa fold the napkins for each place setting.

7. Get your loved one into a day program, the sooner the better. Imagine what you could accomplish in those four to five hours.

8. Be gentle with yourself and forgive yourself for those moments when you are not at your best.

9. Make sure that the kids are aware that this disease is not contagious. Encourage discussions so they do not feel embarrassed to bring friends over. Help allay fears by explaining that medicine and science are working hard to find a treatment and a cure for dementia within their lifetime.

10. Help your child understand that their grandparent's behaviour—be it anger or frustration—is not directed at them. It is part of the disease process, and they will have good days as well as bad days.

11. Perhaps there is a teacher or counsellor who should be made aware of the home situation.

Ideas for activities that children can do with a grandparent who has Alzheimer's:

1. Listen to and sing favourite songs

2. Work on a puzzle together

3. Play a card game or board game with them

4. Read a book to them

5. Watch their favourite TV program or a movie together and share popcorn

6. Colour or draw a picture

7. Bake cookies or do the dishes together

8. Watch a TV program about animals and wildlife—great discussions can come with that.

9. Go for a walk

10. Do stretches and a few light weights for strengthening

11. Make cards, colour them and include a message

12. Make a snack and share it together

13. Go to a park

14. Help fold laundry

15. Feed the birds

Forewarn your children of the continuing decline in their grandparent's condition and discuss placement possibilities if you are thinking in that direction. You are working together as a family to care for a loved one at home for as long as possible, so there should be no surprises.

YOU ARE NOT ALONE.

At the age of seven, my granddaughter, Aspen, asked me whether her grandfather ever talked to her. It shocked me that she had recognized and noted Carl's difficulty in communicating, and reflected on whether she should have a memory of having a conversation with him. Will her memories of him only be found in this book? No, I will speak of the great memories and show her pictures; I will not allow this disease to destroy our memories.

CHAPTER 22

TROUBLES IN THE BATHROOM: YOU'VE GOT THIS

Perhaps you have been in the caregiver role for several years by now. You thought that it could not get any worse, but now you are having to take care of all of your loved one's personal care. How will you cope?

We were not born nurses. We had to learn it. And you can learn to be a caregiver.

You say that you cannot help someone get dressed or washed—really? Watch the caregivers from Home Care. Better yet, get involved with the care, assist them and learn. Become observant, watch and troubleshoot. Take note on how you get dressed, what you wash first during your own shower. Lay on your bed with the pillows in the same position as the caregiver staff do for your loved one. If it fits for you and is comfortable, it might be good for your dearest as well.

You should be able to complete the caring tasks on your own. For example, your loved one spills the entire bowl of soup or chili over themselves. Before you can get to their side, they are rubbing it into their clothes as if they are trying to erase it. You really cannot let them sit in dirty clothes all day while waiting for the next caregiver visit. Learn early in the process because you will need it.

Incontinence

At some point, the majority of people with dementia develop incontinence. When urinary incontinence begins, have your doctor check them for a bladder infection, which could be a cause. Protective pads designed to line underwear are available to absorb small leaks or urgent situations. Depends-type pull-up underwear are available in most stores. These items can become expensive, so discuss this with your Home Care nurse. They often have a plan which discounts the product if your loved one qualifies for it.

Incontinence of stool will happen, and a half-shower, (from the waist down), works best to clean the mess. You can convince them to do it more often than not, and a hand-held shower head is ideal. We address this topic more thoroughly under "Bowel Routine, Constipation and HELP", (below).

Cleanliness is important if and when incontinence becomes a regular and continual issue. Skin care of the genitals and the bum areas needs to be done twice a day, (at minimum), and whenever a bowel movement has occurred. Wash with soap, rinse and pat dry as this is a tender area. Powders can make more of a mess and cause a build-up, which can be harder to clean, so we don't recommend using them. Being in wet underwear will cause an irritation and reddening of the skin, so keeping the area clean and dry, and using a diaper rash ointment, (e.g., Penaten), will help healing take place. Make sure that you wash and dry the areas thoroughly, get in those folds and creases, and remove the irritant.

Bowel Routine, Constipation and HELP

The brain of people with dementia eventually does not recognize the urge to have a bowel movement. It does not recognize the tummy cramps as a time to sit on the toilet. This leads to incontinence or holding back and becoming constipated.

Sometimes they might poop in the shower, the garbage can or on the floor of the bathroom. Then they might want to pick up the poop and push it down the sink drain. Now there is a mess on the floor, the light switch, the walls, clothing, towels and who knows what else they may have touched! We know that it sounds gross, but we need to give you a heads up that it might happen.

Tip: Gloves are important whenever you are caring for your loved one, not just when dealing with incontinence.

Emergency bag: This should consist of a change of clothes, lots of paper towels, garbage bags, disinfectant cleaning solution, disposable wipes, (do not flush these wipes, use the garbage bag), a box of disposable gloves, a fingernail brush, a hand towel, face cloths. This emergency bag should be at the ready all the time.

Tip: If odours bother you, wear a mask and place a dry, unused black tea bag in the mask around your mouth and nose area.

This will nullify odours remarkably well. Add the masks and tea bags to your emergency bag.

If a mess occurs, remove the dirty clothes, clean your loved one's body while they wash their hands **at least twice**. Then one more time using the fingernail brush. Once they are clean and dressed, escort them out of the messy area and settle them in front of the TV, or with a picture book to look at. Then you get to return and finish cleaning the mess and put the laundry on.

Establishing a bowel routine is difficult with their changing diet and decreasing activity. To prevent constipation, you can:

- ❑ Increase their water intake

- ❑ Offer high fibre foods like oatmeal or bran flakes for breakfast, bran muffins for a snack or increase their fruit, (especially figs or prunes), and raw vegetable intake.

- ❑ Make your own fruit laxative, which is easy, economical and handy.

Fruit laxative recipe

This fruit laxative is safe for anyone who needs help with regularity. We suggest two tablespoons daily.

1 cup of chopped dried figs

1 cup of chopped dried prunes

1 cup of raisins

Add apple or orange juice to cover the fruit and bring to a boil, then lower the heat and let simmer for about thirty minutes. Pour this mixture in the blender or food processor and blend until the consistency of a jam. You may need to add a little more juice to achieve the desired consistency. This mixture can be served over toast or eaten off a spoon.

Add a stool softener. Discuss with the pharmacist or doctor. An example of a stool softener pill is Colace. This is not a laxative; it draws water into the stool making it easier for the stool to pass through the body.

Developing a routine of sitting on the toilet at a regular time of day can be difficult. If constipation occurs try the following.

Herbal method: In the later afternoon or early evening, serve them a cup of senna tea for next morning relief. Fill a tea ball with senna leaves, (a dry leaf product that you can order online or pick up at health food stores). Place the tea ball in a cup of boiling water and let it steep for fifteen minutes. Then, remove the tea ball, add honey to taste and serve.

Senna increases the movement of stool through the bowel. Senna leaves are the cheapest method, and they are safe and effective. You can also add the senna tea as the liquid ingredient, (instead of juice), in the fruit laxative recipe. This will make it more effective especially as your loved one becomes less active.

Liquids and pills: Be cautious with all laxatives. Read the list of ingredients and recommendations prior to using. Discuss the issue of constipation with your family doctor and heed their advice.

Colace, (docusate sodium), is a stool softener that works by absorbing water into the stool thereby softening it and easing its passage. It may take one to three days to be effective.

Restoralax is a powdered form of stool softener and laxative. It is to be mixed with water and results are expected in one to three days.

Senokot is a stool softener and laxative pill made from the senna leaf and is available in various forms. For example, Senokot plus a stool softener, Extra Strength Senokot, Senokot with ginger, and Senokot syrup.

Physicians may recommend a combination of medication.

If the stool softeners and laxatives are not effective, you may need to consider a suppository or an enema.

A suppository is a cone-shaped, medication-filled, object which melts or dissolves once inserted in the rectum. Follow the instructions on the box/package. Results are expected in fifteen to sixty minutes. Examples of suppositories are Dulcolax and Glycerine.

An enema is a prefilled, disposable, squeezable plastic bottle containing a solution to induce a bowel movement. Follow instructions on the box/packaging. An example is called Fleet Enema.

Both suppositories and enemas are designed for use as occasional constipation relief. You should understand the instructions and cautions of each product.

If a fecal impaction has occurred, (when they are so constipated that nothing is effective and the stool is hard and stuck), discuss this situation with your Home Care case manager. A health professional may need to do a finger sweep to clear the lower bowel. This procedure is called a manual extraction, and it is a painful procedure.

It is easier to prevent constipation than it is to treat it. Bowel care is a fine balance. If you overtreat constipation, it may result in diarrhea.

Tip: To effectively remove odours from a room, pour a half inch or an inch of fresh, unused coffee grounds into a shallow dish, (such as a pie plate), and leave this dish in the room. Throw out the grounds when they are no longer effective. This not only works well but also does not "over perfume" the air as is the case with many air fresheners.

CHAPTER 23

NAKEDNESS AND SEXUALLY INAPPROPRIATE BEHAVIOUR

Bonds may form in Nursing Homes between residents.

I was asked to be the POA for an elderly lady with no close relatives. I felt honoured to be asked and took my responsibilities seriously. At the time, she was living in an assisted living home. She was coping fairly well although had begun to show increasing signs of memory loss.

One day I received a call from the home telling me that it was time to move my friend to a memory care unit. Apparently, she had appeared for breakfast in the dining room stark naked! It caused quite a commotion amongst the residents. She was a staunch church-going lady, and here she was in all her glory. She would have been mortified. I still wonder how she managed to get so far in this huge facility, and not been stopped by a staff member or fellow resident. Anyway, this began the search for a memory care unit in a nursing home.

Nakedness

The reason people with dementia often take off their clothes is not known. There are theories: uncomfortable clothes, room temperature, are they too hot? Do they have a urinary tract infection which could encourage them to remove their clothing in order to scratch themselves? Perhaps they need a wash and dry underwear because they have been sweating and it is causing irritation, (e.g., jock itch).

To avoid the embarrassment of them removing their clothes in public, bring a shawl, cape or poncho for a quick cover-up. Make it part of your emergency kit along with the wipes, clean underwear and disposable gloves. Blankets or capes are also excellent to have around if this behaviour occurs while the grandchildren are present. It will allow you to relocate the kids while you sort out the nakedness.

Remember, if you approach the situation with anger or frustration, the children will likely remember your response more than remembering that Grandpa was doing something silly.[17] Request that your loved one follow you to the bedroom so you can help them get dressed again. You can try a gentle but firm voice and say, "NO. Stop! In this house we keep our clothes on! Now let's get you dressed and warm."

If nakedness becomes a repetitive behaviour, try altering their clothes to items with buttons up the back or ties that are more difficult to reach and manoeuvre. Have a robe handy in the house for a quick cover and explain that keeping their clothes on will actually help their skin stay clean, so fewer showers! Bonus!

Sexually Inappropriate Behaviour

This topic includes public nudity, masturbation in public, disrobing, inappropriate comments or sexually touching others. The individual with dementia cannot differentiate between what is right or appropriate, and what is not. Because of dementia, they cannot keep their urges in check. This occurs more often in men than women.

Remind them that this behaviour is not acceptable. Be consistent and firm. While shaking your head no, raise your flat hand up and forward indicating stop. Say, "No, stop. I don't like that!" They can read your body language so, by shaking your head and frowning, you will reinforce your message to stop this behaviour.

In many cases, the sexual drive remains as strong as in their earlier years. It is well-documented that venereal diseases amongst the elderly are rising significantly due to sexual relations even in Nursing Homes.

A nursing friend, who works in a Nursing Home, shared stories of finding patients in compromising situations all the time. She never knew what she would find when entering a room. Frequent fights broke out when one partner felt the other had been unfaithful, or was seduced by another resident.

CHAPTER 24

LIVING ALONE WITH DEMENTIA AND WHEN DEMENTIA BRINGS OUT A FIRST LANGUAGE

There are increasing numbers of immigrants arriving in Canada, and many of them do not speak English or French. This can create a problem when they need support and don't have any family around.

A friend of mine checked on an elderly man and found maggots growing on the meat in his sink. He told her that he was thawing it for dinner. No one knows how long it had been thawing, and with limited and decreasing vision, he did not notice the maggots.

A diagnosis of Dementia does not mean that you cannot live alone. On March 6, 2020, St John's Senior Living and Care, (www.stjohnsliving.org), reported that an estimated one-third of people with dementia live alone. They may successfully live alone, but they still need assessments and assistance because they are unlikely to recognize their own disease process and limitations.

Perhaps you may want to organize welfare check. Seven neighbours working together as a team, can each take one day of the week and do a morning and evening check on this person. Bring a coffee or bowl of soup with you; this will give you the excuse for entering the house. Do a quick scan on the state of cleanliness of the house. Place the soup in the fridge and again do a check. Is there food in the fridge? Is it well past expiry? Is mould, (or worse!), growing on items?

Do an assessment of the individual: Are their clothes dirty? Are they forgetting to bathe or comb their hair? Are they speaking clearly or is finding the right word difficult? Are they edgy, irritable or downright cranky? Be aware that the risk for loneliness, depression and social isolation increases for individuals living alone.

Locating the senior's prescription bottle for medications will give you their doctor's name. You may call that physician's office and relay your findings and concerns, even requesting that they contact and notify the next of kin. Perhaps suggest to the family that a Home Care assessment would be in order. If you have the time, ask that you be allowed to be present during the Home Care assessment, (if agreed to by the next of kin), so that you can reinforce and remind the individual of the plan, because they will forget.

The doctor will need to assess the individual to ensure that an Advanced Directive, Code Status and Green Sleeve have been completed. Of course, a diagnosis needs to be made. Does this person have a driver's license which needs to be revoked? Someone needs to be observant for elder abuse.

Alzheimers.ca has a wealth of information listed under the topic of "Dementia and Living Alone," including assessment plans and guides to ease the decision-making process. There are tips and recommendations to ensure that a senior living alone with dementia is safe and comfortable.

Your continued daily visits would be of great help until the next of kin have made decisions. Isn't this what we call a community effort? In the meantime, share your soup or casserole with them and smile. You probably just made their day!

First language isolation

Think ahead and make a list of translators and their phone numbers. The local hospital may also keep a list of translators. Perhaps they could relay a message to an appropriate translator who could contact you. There are translator apps. available for mobile devices.

Pictorial stroke communication charts are available online, or can easily be made with picture cut outs. Even hand-drawn images will assist with communicating needs or requests. You may find examples of these charts at www.basicneedcommunicationboard.com.

Put the word out to family, friends and neighbours that you are searching for a specific translator. You might be surprised by how much help you get. General information on dementia is available in multiple languages at www.alzheimersassociation.ca.

The majority of our communication is non-verbal, so be observant to body language, gestures and facial expressions. Interpreting this behaviour may assist in predicting what the individual is trying to communicate.

One afternoon Carl walked toward me and asked, "Where is my shrimp?" After confirming that he wanted shrimp for a snack, I set off to prepare it. I served it to him saying, "Here is your shrimp, Dear." He became instantly frustrated and said, "No, not that shrimp!" His anxiety was quickly rising as he waved his hands and shook his head from side to side.

"It's OK," I said, "we can figure this out. Show me what it is you want."

He calmed down and walked with me to the garage where he pointed to where his pipe was supposed to be. Ahh yes, we found the pipe and he also enjoyed his shrimp appetizer.

CHAPTER 25

THE DISEASE PROGRESSES

Inevitably this disease takes away the ability to move around and will result in your loved one becoming bedridden. This brings a lot of other problems, so here are some suggestions to maker life a little easier.

Skin care and positioning

This is a taxing stage of the disease, and not everyone will be able to cope with it. They may be forced to consider moving their loved one into a nursing home.

One morning, Carl did not have the strength to get out of bed and I could not lift him. The disease had advanced. He became quieter, slept more, gradually began choking more, would only take soft foods and then that decreased as well. His care needs changed.

Now is the time to rent a hospital bed as it allows for easier positioning, and raising the head of bed reduces the chances of choking on liquids or aspirations. Your Home Care nurse can help organize this.

Once bedridden, your loved one will need to be repositioned from side to back to side every three hours around the clock, with a back rub and ankle/heel care at every turn. Any area in contact with the bed will get red and will need to have the pressure relieved, (by turning and repositioning). The skin must be massaged as well to encourage circulation and healing, in order to prevent skin breakdown.

Pillows should be used extensively and will help relieve some of the pressure on bony areas, as well as maintain proper body alignment. How many pillows? I had eight available and consistently used six.

When positioned on a side, a pillow is placed under the upper arm. Two to three pillows keep the upper leg elevated, and in good line with the body, to prevent pressure areas to the lower leg. Slightly bend both legs to relieve stress on the knee joints, and position the legs so that they are not on top of each other. Now place at least two pillows behind them, to prevent them from rolling back.

If their shoulder is tucked behind them, slide your arm under that shoulder and pull it, without pulling on the elbow. This will allow them to lean back a little, and release the weight and pressure on their shoulder. It will also prevent a potential pressure area.

And, of course, a pillow for under the head. When lying on their back, try a pillow under each arm. Bend the arm a little at the elbow and elevate the entire arm on a pillow. (Marg calls it making an angel wing!). This position is comfortable, prevents pressure on the elbow, and makes breathing easier, because it reduces the weight on the chest muscles.

When lying on their back, you should raise each leg on a pillow and keep the heel off the bed. Do not use socks on their feet, because you cannot assess what you cannot see. Keeping their feet bare will allow you to check those heels and ankles, and massage them with every turn.

Pay attention to how the Home Care workers position and place pillows.

Try the pillow positioning on yourself. If it is comfortable for you, then rest assured it will be comfortable for them as well.

Tip: Elevate the head of the bed about fifteen degrees to help prevent choking and aspirations. Elevate it higher when you are offering food and fluids, in order to facilitate swallowing, and reduce choking episodes. Elevate the foot of the bed a little to help prevent them from sliding down the bed, because lifting them back up is a two-person job.

My special time with Carl was the daily bed bath, a personal ritual and opportunity to gently massage lotions into his skin. That was followed by a daily linen change with the help of my Home Care worker.

Skin breakdown is difficult to treat, and it is far easier to prevent than it is to cure. Concentrate your skin care regimens on those red areas, shoulders, low back, heels and ankles.

Pressure sores can quickly occur, are difficult to treat, and can leave draining open sores which can easily get infected.

In the event of skin breakdown or a wound, please call your Home Care nurse for advice as there are many treatments available. However, these treatments are dependent on the type and the location of the wound. Please do not try home-based remedies without an assessment, because you can do more harm than good.

A shampoo will require help, but if you put the shampoo on before you change the linens, it will be much easier! Have a pile of towels ready and a basin to collect the rinse water. Dry shampoos are available at pharmacies; they absorb the oils but do not actually clean the scalp, or hair.

Fingernail and toenail care can be done as needed, and in the same manner as you clean, trim and file your own nails.

Tip: Shaves are easy with an electric razor. It is worth the investment.

Having completed the morning care, you will probably want to freshen their looks with a clean shirt, and to be ready for company.

I did not have hospital gowns to dress Carl in, so I cut along the centre of the back of a T-shirt, all the way up to the collar. The shirt then easily slid over his head, and with the back of the shirt cut open, it was easy to place his arms through the sleeves. Then a little tuck or roll of the shirt on the side and he looked wonderful.

Changing linens/sheets

Another two-person job is changing the linens on the bed. Follow the care worker's lead. You might elect to play some soft, relaxing music and dim the lights in the room, to encourage peacefulness and calm.

We recommend a daily bed bath once they become bedridden, because you cannot assess what you cannot see. The only way you will notice the reddened areas, or the beginning of the skin breaking down, is by washing, drying and massaging these bony areas. Have a close look, and take advantage of this opportunity, to gently and slowly massage their arms, hands, back, shoulders and feet. Notice how they relax.

The procedure:

With help and with the bed flat, lift and position your loved one on their side close to the elevated side rail.

One person holds and supports the person on their side.

The other person undoes the bottom sheet and rolls it snugly, and tucks it just beneath the bedridden person.

Now is a great time to wash the upper back and bum, and give a back rub, paying attention to any pressure areas.

A double thickness of heavy-duty poly, about five feet long and six feet wide is added, making sure that you have about one foot of poly overhanging the mattress. This layer of poly is important because it allows you to lift, slide and reposition the person. Roll the excess poly snugly and tuck it with the clean bottom sheet.

Add a large beach towel next to make sure that no skin will come in contact with the poly, otherwise moisture and heat can lead to skin breakdown. Roll the extra width of the towel in a snug log and tuck again.

For the last layer, add a large, quilted, waterproof incontinence pad. I used one that was about five feet long and four feet wide. They are available at some pharmacies and on Amazon. We suggest that you buy two, so that while one is on the bed, the other one is in the laundry. This pad is cushioned, soft and will absorb the body's heat and even a leaky diaper. Again, roll the extra portion and tuck.

The act of rolling them over the bump or log, may create fear and have them reaching out and grabbing at the first thing that they come in contact with. To prevent injuries, take their hand or allow them to grab and hang on to your wrist while the turn is completed.

Before rolling the person over all of these rolls, make the rolls as thin as possible and keep them snug. Together you roll the person over all the layers and rolls, and the side that you freshly washed will now be lying on the clean quilted pad.

Now it is your turn to hold and support your loved one, while your helper removes the dirty layer and straightens the clean layers.

You MUST make sure to pull each layer snugly and remove the folds, wrinkles and creases, as lumps and bumps will increase the pressure areas.

Now you finish the bath by washing the top side, do skin care, massage those pressure areas and reposition.

The repositioning is done by rolling the layers, (poly, towel and quilted pad), together snugly, and then lifting and sliding the poly. Do not pull or push on the person. All positioning is done by lifting and sliding the poly and upper layers of the towel and quilted pad.

If turning on a side, have the pillows for the back ready for tucking behind them.

If you are caring for a heavy person, you may need a double layer of poly to ensure that it is strong enough to handle their weight.

Home Care workers are excellent at performing these duties and are a valuable asset. Follow their lead and ask them to teach you, and to explain the reasoning for their actions.

Mouth care

Mouth care can easily be done using a toothette swab. It is a piece of coloured foam, stuck to a lollipop type of stick. They are available at most pharmacies and Walmart. Dip the foam end of the swab in a freshly-poured ounce of Club Soda. Then gently brush their gums and teeth. The Club Soda is effective at cutting through, and dissolving that mucus layer that will accumulate over their teeth. They may wish to suck on the foam, which is fine as it will help dissolve any build up of mucous in the mouth.

If you wish to increase or encourage fluid intake, try dipping a clean toothette in ginger ale. While they bite down and suck on the ginger ale swab, you can continue to brush with the Club Soda. If they really bite down on the swab, don't pull on it to remove it, as you may break off a chunk of foam. Just keep brushing with the first swab and soon they will release their grip and you will be able to remove it.

Dentures need to be removed, brushed and rinsed then reinserted. Ensure that the dentures or partial plates are firmly positioned and not floating in their mouth.

Breathing changes

Once bedridden, the fluids in the body tend to move and shift. During the day, with the head of the bed elevated, fluids will tend to pool toward the legs and feet. This may be seen as swelling. At night with the bed flatter, the fluids get reabsorbed in the bloodstream and can get moved to the lungs. This can cause wet, rattly breathing sounds. Sometimes this wet breathing is accompanied by weak coughs and perhaps a wheeze, or squeaky sound during breathing.

This fluid in the lungs can cause a decrease in the oxygen level, which is detected by the brain and wakes them up frequently during the night. The brain is saying, "Hey, wake up! Your oxygen is low. Wake up and breathe more." If this occurs, try elevating the head of the bed. The excess fluid will settle to the lower lung area, allowing the oxygen level to improve in the upper and mid areas of the lungs. The problem is momentarily solved. Perhaps call the Home Care nurse in the morning, describe these events and follow their directions.

Pain management

I heard the deep guttural moans whenever I turned Carl. He had arthritic pain before the disease and took over-the-counter pain medication daily. He was quickly cut off from the pain management because he was not able to swallow. I believe that he felt pain.

Throughout his experience with Alzheimer's, he frequently rubbed his temples, complained of "sparks" in his head and occasionally had headaches. After discussing this with our family doctor, he remained on an over-the-counter painkiller. When he could no longer swallow, the deep moaning and groaning started with every movement and repositioning. It is a deep heart-breaking sound, so I called the doctor to get him stronger pain medication.

There are two trains of thought on pain in Alzheimer's and Dementia individuals. Some people believe they do not experience or sense pain and others, (us included), who believe they definitely do.

You can also call the Home Care nurse and request an assessment by Palliative nurses. This team will assess, recommend and suggest care information for the management of pain. The Home Care nurse can assist with decisions that you must make, and can support you during this trying time.

Charles was admitted to the hospital for the third and final time shortly before he died. He was clearly in a lot of pain, mainly from the neck fractures and cerebral hemorrhage he had sustained from the fall down the stairs two months earlier. The doctors could see his distress and ordered pain relief to be administered orally, by injection and by a patch. There is absolutely no doubt that he was in severe pain. This was confirmed when the Palliative Care team took over his case, so I do not believe that Alzheimer's and dementia patients do not feel pain.

I am not a particularly religious person, but I remember praying to God on many occasions to take Charles in his sleep. It did not seem right or humane that he was being made to suffer so much. It is perfectly normal to wonder how long your loved one is going to live. It is also normal to wonder if you are going to be able to continue looking after them for much longer, especially when you are physically exhausted and sleep-deprived. So do not be hard on yourself if you have the same thoughts sometimes. It is natural.

CHAPTER 26

POP GOES THE BALLOON

I found myself getting short with most people. I was running out of patience and had difficulty holding my words in check.

One day, a health care worker arrived to assist with the daily linen change and to help reposition Carl.

She stood in the doorway of the bedroom and said, "I have to stay six feet away. How can I help?"

"Well, unless you have really long arms, you may as well go home!" I snapped back.

A minute later, she entered the room and helped me. She explained that due to COVID-19 regulations, she was supposed to maintain a distance of six feet from people not wearing a mask. I was not about to place a mask on myself, or on my dying husband while we were in our own home. If anyone else wished to don a mask, that was fine. If Carl had a moment of clarity, I wanted him to see me and recognize me, so I was therefore not going to hide behind a mask.

Compare yourself to a balloon. It fills and fills with frustrations, fears, anger, sadness and every other emotion. It continues to fill until one day you cannot take it anymore. An event occurs to push you over the edge and the balloon bursts. You lash out, perhaps scream at someone. You take out your anger on those whom you feel are responsible for this outburst.

My friend, Dawn, went to the pharmacy to fill a prescription for her husband. He was at home, bedridden and receiving end-of-life care for cancer. The Pharmacist informed her that the prescription could not be filled without first seeing her husband, in order to make sure that the pills were for him. Well, Dawn lost it! She exploded into yelling because someone was preventing her from doing the only thing she could do to help her husband.

Alan Alda wrote, "Adapt, adjust and revise because, the only thing that you can be sure of is that things change." Realize that you cannot change the person with Alzheimer's, so in order to cope and guide, YOU must change. Adapt to your situation, adjust and revise your thoughts, your plans and your dreams. Deal with today only.

You must learn to let it go and take a deep breath. Let go of the resentment, the frustrations, the anger and those negative emotions because, they are harming you! They increase your stress and your inflammatory response. Practice taking a few deep breaths with slow exhalation because, it will relax you, allow you to gather a little more patience, and get you through this moment. If possible, go for a brisk walk outdoors or if you are unable to leave the home, try jumping jacks, a little cardio workout, marching on the spot, knee bends or stretches—any activity to use up those tense and frustrating feelings. Call family or friends to come over and give you a break.

Your emotions are real and normal. You have reached a roadblock while trying to give end-of-life care to someone you love. You have reached your breaking point. Be gentle with yourself. Keep writing! You must vent and release the pressure trapped inside you, and take a few deep breaths. Then release it and let it go.

COVID-19 restrictions made caring for a loved one more difficult. There was more isolation, fewer people around to give the caregiver a much-needed break, more loneliness, and the rate of caregiver burnout increased.

One evening, while a patient in the hospital, Charles became very restless and developed such violent hiccup, his body would almost lift off the bed with each one. They didn't bother him as much as they did me. I asked his nurse if they could give him medication to stop them. In my nursing days, we would have been able to get hold of a duty 'House Doctor' within minutes, to write a prescription. Now they needed to track down a member of the Palliative Care team, who were working flat out with so many really sick people, who were dying of Covid. Then the prescription needed to be sent to the hospital pharmacy. This meant an almost three hour wait. I found myself getting very angry and upset about this delay. How could this be allowed to happen?

CHAPTER 27

EXPECTED DEATH AT HOME FORM

If you have experienced a 911 call, you will be familiar with all the emergency services who turn up with their flashing lights, and have your neighbours peering out of their windows to see what is going on. In order to have your loved one taken discreetly to the funeral home after death, this is an important chapter to read.

Almost twenty-five years before his death, Charles made arrangements to donate his body to the medical school at the University of Calgary. This was not done to save money for a funeral, as some believed. He felt strongly about medical students having bodies to practice on, and he reminded me frequently that this wish MUST be carried out. He also pre-paid the funeral home for a service to follow his death. This allowed him to have some say in how we would celebrate his life, while also saving the family a lot of money later. I have followed his guidance and have pre-paid my own funeral service, so that my family does not have to worry about that expense when the time comes, which can be overwhelming.

The "Expected Death at Home" form can be obtained from your Home Care nurse or your doctor and must be completed and signed by them. Keep it at home if your wishes are for a calm and peaceful home death. It gives you the legal right to call the funeral home directly following your loved one's death, and arrange for their body to be picked up.

If you elected to not complete the "Expected Death at Home" form, you must call the police and the ambulance. The police are notified in order to disprove foul play and start a report. The ambulance will transport your loved one to the hospital morgue. Once the paperwork and investigation are complete, the body will be released to the funeral home of your choice.

Speaking of funeral homes, plan to call one with your information and requests. They will give you a detailed list of what they will do and the costs for everything. We found the funeral directors to be supportive, empathetic and super helpful.

Death doulas are breaking ground in North America. They offer personalized support to the person dying as well as to the family. The End of Life Doula Association of Canada defines the end of life doula as someone who "empowers, educates and encourages people and their families to be involved in making end of life decisions." They can provide emotional and spiritual support, while following the dying person's wishes, as well as their family's guidance. Rituals, traditions and lifestyles are honoured while maintaining a sense of calm for the dying. There is a charge for this service, and more information is available online at www.deathdoula.ca.[18]

I checked on Carl and found him with tears streaming down his face. I asked him why he was crying and he replied, "I don't know." Did he know that the end was near? Was he tired of this disease? I hugged him and cried with him. This disease really sucks! It is so painful.

CHAPTER 28

END OF LIFE

Not many of us will have witnessed what happens as people near death. This chapter is designed to prepare you ahead of time.

My good friends, Paul and Jackie, took my puppy to their home for an afternoon. This allowed me to concentrate on Carl's state and his care. I did not have to worry about the dog's needs. I felt overwhelmed; this dying process seemed slow to arrive, but now it was happening too quickly. I was not ready to say goodbye.

During the final stages of life, you will notice a major slowing down of all bodily functions.

General weakness. Moving in bed becomes more difficult. Even lifting their arms is difficult. There is a marked decrease in energy.

Decrease in speech and communication. They may appear withdrawn. They can hear you, so don't shout. Speak calmly and know that they are unable to respond. Now is the time for those important last words to your loved one.

Decrease in appetite and less fluid intake. The decrease in appetite begins during the last month of life, and there is more difficulty swallowing. You can use toothettes oral swabs soaked in Club Soda or ginger ale to keep their mouth moist.

Decrease in urine. Because of the decrease in fluid intake, and the fact that the kidneys are beginning to shut down, there will be a marked decrease in the amount of urine produced. The urine will be dark and concentrated.

Increase in sleep. Metabolism decreases and a lack of food and fluids leads to dehydration, which stimulates the brain to produce endorphins. These endorphins induce comfort and promote rest. They will sleep most of the day and night.

Twitches. Sometimes jerky type of muscle twitches occur. These twitches are not painful for them, but they are more difficult for the family to observe.

Breathing changes. Breathing will range from shallow to extra deep, at times irregular with long pauses before the next breath. Rattly, noisy breathing, (death rattle), is common. We call it laboured breathing because, extra effort goes into each breath as more muscles are used, and needed to move the air. Pillows positioned under their arms will facilitate the movement of air, and ease the work of breathing a little.

Heart rate changes. It is normal for the heart rate to slow and become irregular, partly due to the decreasing oxygen levels.

Colour changes. With the circulation decreasing, the available oxygen will be delivered to major organs and blood flow to the extremities will decrease. This causes blotchy, pale and purple discolouration in the feet, legs and hands. This discolouration will continue to become more pronounced as death approaches.

Throughout this book, we stress keeping notes that will be beneficial later when decisions must be made. Well, this is later. You will decide on whether you wish to continue with death at home, or perhaps move to Hospice, Palliative Care or death in a hospital. Hospice and Palliative support teams can come to your home so you do not have to relocate your loved one. Due to their inability to swallow at this time, some physicians may suggest the addition of intravenous fluids. Other physicians may suggest the fluid intake be only via sponges or toothette swabs. Follow the guidance of your Home Care and medical teams.

I chose to not extend the disease. Carl had suffered enough, and our sons felt the same. No feedings in a tube, no intravenous fluids, just a peaceful, restful environment, which is what he wanted. He had told the doctor there were to be no "extras."

These decisions are difficult to make. Read your notes, discuss them with your immediate family, and you will make the decisions without guilt, knowing that you did what had to be done.

Keep the music softly playing, keep the lights low. Make the room as peaceful as possible. Hold their hand, say what needs to be said. It is believed that the sense of hearing is the last to leave our body, so pour it out.

Cultural and/or religious beliefs may dictate that you open a window to allow the soul to be free. Perhaps a final ritualistic bath and body preparation is in order.

Charles was admitted to hospital for a third time, suffering with a high fever and seizures. His GP and Gerontologist were concerned that these side effects were due to the excessive amounts of anti-psychotic drugs that he was receiving. It was during this admission that he was placed under the care of the Palliative Care team, and we agreed that a move to a Hospice center would be very appropriate at this time.

Charles was given medication for his hiccups and it worked surprisingly well. I left the hospital around eleven o'clock that evening. My youngest son was due to come and take over from me, and be with his Dad for the night. Unbeknownst to me, he had tested positive for Covid that afternoon and could not come in to the hospital.

Exhausted from long days of being with Charles in the hospital, I fell into a deep sleep, only to be awakened by my phone ringing in the early hours of the next morning. A nurse informed me that Charles had died twenty minutes ago. There was no 'I am sorry for your loss,' only instructions on when I needed to pick up his belongings the next morning. It was so cold and uncaring, and it has remained in my memory to this day. When did human beings begin to behave in such an uncaring manner?

I felt so upset that none of us were with him when he passed away. I had tried to make sure that someone was with him all the time when he was in the hospital, mainly because he was so confused and scared, but because of that awful Covid outbreak, he died alone.

Some people have told me that it may have been Charles' wish to be alone. I don't know that I necessarily believe that, however I take comfort in knowing that I insisted that he be given medication for those awful hiccups, which would have made him more comfortable.

And so begins your healing journey.

When death of your loved one occurs, you may feel numb, a little lost. And you will feel ever so alone, even if there are others beside you. This is a different loneliness, an empty one. Don't be in a rush, there is time. You don't have to make calls right at this moment. Allow yourself to deep breathe one more time….be present in this moment.

Know that the numb feeling will be replaced by deep sorrow.

The house was quieter. The television was off. Soft music played in the bedroom. The curtains were drawn and the lights were dimmed. Puppy slept quietly under Carl's hospital bed. I felt alone. Empty. Drained. A heavy weight was bearing down on me. I did not know how I would cope.

CHAPTER 29

THEN WHAT?

"Grief is the price we pay for love." - Queen Elizabeth II

Suddenly, the house is silent. You still can't wrap your head around the situation. You feel numb. It is going to take you some time. There is no rush. No matter how prepared, you will still experience shock. We offer a few tips to help you. There are no rules about bereavement.

About a month after Carl's passing, I had a doctor's appointment and as I sat in the waiting room, I could hear the receptionist's beautiful accent. That same accent that was always there when I needed advice or to speak to the doctor. That was my trigger, the tears flooded non-stop, I was sobbing.

My sons said, "We lost Dad twice. Once to Alzheimer's and then, to physical death." Both deaths were extremely painful for them to be a part of. I am so thankful for their love and support.

We assume that the "Expected Death at Home" form has been completed, so at some point you will call the funeral home, with whom you have made arrangements to transport your loved one.

Then the emptiness really sets in. Everything is different, routines change, there is no one to talk to, share things with. Even the house is different. You could swear that sometimes it echoes. There is no longer any rush to complete or accomplish anything. And you will cry at the drop of a pin. Where are these tears coming from? Whenever it happens, know that you are normal. Your emotions are still on that roller coaster ride. Keep writing those notes.

Funeral homes will likely give you a list of duties and a timeline to follow to accomplish them. Their help is invaluable. Amongst other things, they will apply to the government for the $2500 you are eligible to receive for funeral costs. Please note you are required to pay tax on that money.

Life insurance companies or your financial advisor should be notified of the death. The policies are often paid out quickly.

There is no immediate rush to contact the banks, but at some point, you should notify them in order to remove a name from an account, or to close an account. However, if you have a balance owing on joint credit cards, those will be frozen until they have been paid in full.

You must notify the government as soon as possible. If CPP and OAS payments have been received, the date of death will be the cut-off date. If you have received money until the end of the month following the death, the government will ask for it back.

Other decisions include funeral or celebration of life, passport, etc. All in due time. There is no rush.

When all the busy-ness is over, when the flowers begin to wilt, the friends have gone and you are alone, you will feel a host of emotions. Anger may be present because this was not the retirement that you had planned. Frustration because why did this stupid disease happen to our loved one? Loneliness, sadness and emptiness all at once. Be gentle with yourself. These emotions are normal. Allow yourself to feel. You may feel guilt—did I do the right thing? Should I have done more? Could I have done more? Did I give good care?

You did all that you could. You could not have given more. Be gentle, re-read your notes to reaffirm that you did all that you could.

Grief

Grief is very personal. Each person handles it differently, and there is no right of wrong way.

Dementia is such a cruel disease because it is akin to losing your loved one twice. As you watch their shrinking brains remove their ability to recognize and communicate with you, you mourn the loss of that wonderful, vibrant person you loved so much. And then you get to do it again when they finally give up the battle and die.

The duration of the grieving experience varies, as does the experience itself. It is dependent on a few factors:

1. Your relationship with the person who died. How close were you?

2. The circumstances of the death. Is there guilt or regret involved?

3. Your own life experiences. How do you cope with tragedy and sadness?

It is said that grief has five stages:

1. Denial/isolation: emotional shut-down, avoid others, fear, shock, numbness.

2. Anger: frustration, anxiety, loneliness, uncertainty, preoccupied with thoughts of loved one.

3. A search for meaning: Struggling to understand why this loss happened.

4. Depression: feeling overwhelmed, helpless, hostile, extremely sad and withdrawing.

5. Acceptance: comes with adjusting to daily life without your loved one; coming to terms and accepting the loss.[19]

Helping a grieving person

1. Reach out, show that you care, allow venting and sharing.

2. Find ways to help so that life does not become overwhelming to the grieving person. Housework, yard work, meals, laundry. Avoid vague offers like "Let me

know if you need anything." Be specific: "I will bring dinner on Wednesday."

3. Listen. Everyone experiences grief differently. They are probably not looking for advice, so just be there, listen, allow them to speak.

4. Do not offer your personal experience with loss at this time; today's emotion is not yours.

5. Avoid comments that turn the situation like, "You are lucky that you still have your mom," or, "Be grateful for what you have." Although these positive comments have good intentions, they can make the grieving person feel that their grief is not valid. Telling someone in pain that their pain could certainly have been worse is neither effective nor helpful.[20]

You will heal, and in time the pain will lessen, as a renewed sense of meaning and purpose will dominate. Be grateful that they are no longer suffering, and can be at peace. Of course, we miss them but we do not wish that they could still be with us under those circumstances.

Time is needed to come to terms with everything that has happened. There will be tears as we remember all the things that we loved and miss about them. Our first Christmas without them, their birthday, our birthday, wedding anniversaries, and so on. We recommend that you surround yourself with family and friends, or take a wonderful trip which you can look forward to, and help you make new memories while not forgetting the past.

Grief counseling can be helpful if you need the extra support. Local churches and some hospitals provide this type of service.

You have completed a monumental journey of caring for your loved one through all the stages of a disease for which there is currently no cure.

Look back on all that you have accomplished with pride.

Do not have regrets or question how you might have handled situations differently.

You did all that you could to honour your loved one as best as you could, given the circumstances.

Now is the time to focus on you.

Be kind to yourself and take time to become a new version of yourself.

ADDITIONAL RESOURCES

Alive Inside - Documentary Michael Rossato-Bennett, Producer & Director.
Dan Cohen, Social Worker and Project Manager

Alzheimer Association of Canada

Alzheimers.org.uk

Dementia Home Care, "How to Prepare Before, During and After" by Cram Perkins

Alzheimer's Through the Stages "What to Expect, What to Say, What to Do" by Mary Moller, MSW, CAS

Caregiving Both Ways - A guide to Caring for a Love one with Dementia (and Yourself) by Molly Wisinewski

Toolkit for Caregivers - Tips, Skills and Wisdom to Maximize Your Time Together by Deirdre Edwards

Brain Health Breakthrough: episode transcripts hosted by Peggy Sarlin and featuring the following guest speakers:

1. Dr. Dale Bredesen
2. Dr. Heather Sandison
3. Dr. Kat Toups

4. Dr. Sid O'Bryant
5. Dr. Roberta Brinton
6. Dr. David Perlmutter
7. Dr. Melissa Batchelor
8. Dr. Ryan Greene
9. Dr. Daniel Stickler
10. Dr. David Haase

ACKNOWLEDGMENTS

Marg thanks Dana, Jackie, Paul and Dawn for their help and friendship.

Conrad and April, Brian and Chantelle: family is everything. Thanks for your help, support and for finding humour when I could not.

Dr Logan thank you for the care you provided for Carl.

Caroline thanks Mark and Ben, my incredible sons, for all their help and support, especially during the last year of Dad's life. Thank you.

Thank you to Vytality at Home co-founders. Brad Lohman makes sure that each of their clients is perfectly matched to their Caregivers. He even missed part of a hockey game when I needed extra help in an emergency. Nicole Dyer takes care of hiring the staff and has the unenviable job of scheduling everyone and handling all the accounting. Thank you so much.

To Jonathon and Annette, Caregivers with Vytality at Home, for all the countless hours you helped us look after Charles. We could not have coped without you. Thank you.

INDEX

A

Adapt, adjust and revise 135
Advanced directive 43, 121
Adult day program 98
Aggression 8, 80
Agnosia 69
Air pollution 22
Alcohol 23
'Alive Inside' you-tube video 84
Alternating pressure mattress 36
Alzheimer's 2
Alzheimer's Association 46
Amyloid plaques 3
Angel wing positioning 125
Anger 8, 71, 83
Anxiety 11, 80
Aspiration 15, 124
ApoE gene 3
Assessments 18

B

Balance 51
Balanced diet 25, 101
Bed-bath/shampoo 127
Bells on door knobs 57
Bedridden 124
Behavior 2, 8, 18
Blister pack 91
Blood sugar 21
Bowel routine 112
Bracelet (dementia) 57
Brain bleeds 19
Brain exercises 26
Breathing 24, 125, 141

C

Canada caregiver credit 44
Canes and walkers 52, 87
Carbohydrates 25
Caregiver 65
Changing sheets/linens 127
Chipmunk cheeks 89
Choking 9, 90

Cholesterol and fats 3
Christmas lights 78
Circadian rhythm 81
Code status 121
Cognitive decline 2
Color changes 141
Communication 2, 8
Confusion 8, 80
Connections 1
Constipation 112
Coordination 13
Creutzfeldt Jakob Disease 5
CT scan 19

D
Daily activities 8
Deep breathing 24, 106, 135
Degenerative disorder 5
Dehydration 15, 18
Dementia 2, 8
Dementia bracelet 57
Depression 24
Department Motor Vehicles 94
Designated supportive living 36
Diabetes 21
Difficulty thinking 2
Dignity 31
Diphenhydramine 23
Dosettes 91
Drivers license 94

E
Early onset Alzheimer's 3
Elder abuse 59
Electrolyte imbalance 18
Emergency care bag 112
Endogenous 22
Enema 115
Examinations 18
Executive function 2, 12
Exogenous 22
Expected death at home form 138, 145

F
Falls 4, 15
Family history 18
Fats and cholesterol 3
Fecal impaction 116
Fidget sleeve, apron or blanket 75
Fight or flight 69
First language 122
Flavor additives 22
Forgetful 8
Frontotemporal Dementia 4
Fruit laxative recipe 113

Funeral home 138
Frustrations 8, 42, 71

G
Galantamine 27
Genes 3
Genetics 3
Gerontologist 20, 27, 34, 49
Gout 22
Green sleeve 43, 121
Grief counselling 149
Guns and ammunition 51

H
Hallucinations 4
Headphones 85, 86
Head trauma 4, 23
Heart rate changes 141
Heavy duty poly 128
Home care 34, 46, 98, 126, 142
Hormones 3
Hospice care 38, 142
Huntington disease 4
Hypertension 25

I
Impaired brain function 2
Immune system 25
Inappropriate 8
Incontinence 111
Incontinent pad for bed 129
Independence 35
Indigenous Medicine Wheel 32
Infections 15, 18
Inflammatory response 23, 135
Injury 4
Insulin resistance 21

K
Kidney stones 22
Knives 51

L
Lack of activity 22
Lack of sensitivity 8
Language 4, 122
Lecanemab 28
Let it go 42, 135
Lewy Body Dementia 4
Loneliness 24
Long Term Care 36
Loss of focus 4

M
Malnutrition 15
Medications 50, 54, 66
Medicine Wheel 32

Memory loss 2, 8, 18
Mental function 8
Mild cognitive 7
Mindfulness 23
Mini mental test 19
MoCA test 19
Mood swings 14
Mouth care and mouth swabs 130, 141
MP3 player 85
MRI 19
Multigenerational home 105
Multiple sclerosis 5

N
Nakedness 117
Neurons 2, 3

O
Obsessive/compulsive 73
Odor management 113, 116
Oxygen 22

P
Pain management 132
Palliative care 38, 143
Parkinson's Disease 5
Path of Dementia 33
Patterned plates 89
Person-centered care 31
Personal care 36
Personality 8
Plaques (amyloid) 3
Pneumonia 15
Poor judgement 8
Positioning 124
Positive attitude 26
Power of attorney 44
Preservatives 22
Pressure mattress 36
Pressure sores 126
Private Nursing Homes 36, 39
Problem solving 4
Processed meats 25
Purine 22

Q
Quality of life 18, 38

R
Reasoning 2
Refined carbohydrates 25
Relaxation 23
REM sleep 22
Remembering 2
Repetitive behavior 11, 74
Respect 31
Respite 47, 101
Resuscitated 43

Rigidity 4
Run-away plan 49

S
Safety checks 35
Safety transfer belt 53
Sandwich generation 105
Security system 57
Sedatives 23
Senna leaves 114
Sexually inappropriate 117
Siderails 35
Sleep apnea 22
Slow thinking 4
Smart watch 50
Social circle 24
Social skills 15
Spirituality 38
Sports injuries 4
Statistics 1
Sticky proteins
Stress 23
Strokes 19
Stool softener 114
Sundowning 80
Sunshine lamp 82
Support group 103
Suppository 115
Suspicious 8
Swallowing 9, 126

T
Tactless 8
Tao tangles 3
Task management 7
Thiamine 5
Timeline 18
Toxins 22
Translator 22
Traumatic Brain Injury 4
Tremors 4
Trial drugs 27
Trouble shooting 73, 87, 110
Trust your gut 19
Tumors 19
Twitches 141

U
Uric acid 21

V
Vascular dementia 4
Ventilator 43
Violence 72
Visual perception 3
Vitamin 5

W
Walkers, canes 52, 87
Wandering 8, 13, 55, 80

Weakness 140
Weapons 51
Welfare checks 121
Wernicke Korsakoff
  Syndrome 5
White board 12, 46
Will 44
Witching hour 81

Y
Yelling 41, 72, 81, 135
Yoga 23

ENDNOTES

1. Alzheimer Society of Canada website
2. Mayo Clinic Website
3. Stages of Alzheimer's, Alzheimer's.org 2023
4. National Institute on Aging, nia.nih.gov
5. https://www.alz.org
6. Dr. Roberta Diaz, university of Arizona Health Sciences
7. Alzheimer's Association https:www.alz.org>dementia
8. https://www.nia.nih.gov
9. https://www.michaeljfox.org
10. Dr. David Perlmutter, Associate professor University of Miami and Neurologist.
11. Dr. Daniel Stickler, MD and CEO of the Apeiron Center for Human Potential.
12. Dr. Daniel Stickler (as above)
13. Dr. Ryan Greene, Indiana University School of Medicine
14. Dr. Sid O'Bryant, University of North Texas professor and executive director. Nov. 2022
15. Alzheimer Association, alz.org
16. National Institute of Neurological Disorders and Stroke
17. Tracy Cram Perkins, Dementia Home Care, Behler Publications 2021, page 107
18. End of Life Doula Association of Canada.org, Help People Live.
19. Webmd.com, Normal Grieving and Stages of Grief.
20. How to Help Someone that is Grieving, Cancercare.org.

ABOUT THE AUTHORS

Each night, after we had settled our husbands in bed, we would chat on the phone for around 45 minutes, sharing everything that had happened during the day. Sometimes we laughed and sometimes we cried. Often we would make suggestions on how to cope with a new situation that had arisen. We both looked forward to those chats.

We decided to share our experiences with other families who are currently, or who will in the near future be, facing this journey. We hope our book will be of help to you.